LAKE MINNETONKA INSIGHTS

Discovery and Legends

James W. Ogland

Copyright © 2010 James William Ogland
All rights reserved
First edition

Cover: *Express Boat Minnehaha* postcard 1910
Back cover: *Souvenir Booklet* 1909

All postcards are from the authors personal collection unless otherwise specified
The text and graphics design are by the author

Printed in USA

This book may not be reproduced in whole or in part, by any means, electronic or mechanical, including photocopying, recording, or by any information storage and retrieval system, (with the exception of short quotes for the purpose of review), without permission in writing from the publisher. For further information, address DNALGO Publications, Box 935 Wayzata, Minnesota 55391-1008.

FIRST IMPRESSION AUGUST 1, 2010
ISBN 978-0-615-38047-6
August 1, 2010

Ogland, James W.
    Lake Minnetonka Postcards and vintage photos / by
    James W. Ogland, — 1st edition

CONTENTS

INTRODUCTION II

PREFACE III

EARLY HISTORY IV

INSIGHTS 1

TIME LINE 3

HOTELS 13

STEAMBOATS 23

EXCELSIOR 33

WAYZATA 43

YACHTING 53

MOUND 63

BIG ISLAND 73

MINNEHAHA 83

POSTCARDS 93

INDEX TO PAGES 101

INTRODUCTION... *a brief overview*

DISCOVERY

LAKE MINNETONKA is located in central Minnesota and is just west of the Twin Cities of Minneapolis and St. Paul. It was a favorite place of the early American Indian. They called it "mi-ni-tan-ka," *a great place of water or big water.* In 1822 two young boys from nearby Fort Snelling decided to go exploring. They began their outing at a beautiful waterfall, later named Minnehaha Falls. Canoeing up the stream that supplied the falls, they soon discovered that it went farther than anyone had previously realized. After paddling most of the day along its twisting, turning, and meandering path through dense woods and over sparse prairie grass, *they made an astonishing discovery.* The little creek that they had been following flowed from the most beautiful lake that anyone could imagine. It was a deep blue, and the breeze blowing across it was cool and refreshing. The sun glinted and sparkled on every wave. There were islands, peninsulas and many bays, large and small, all connected to each other. It was an unexpected, awesome sight. *It was the discovery of Lake Minnetonka.*

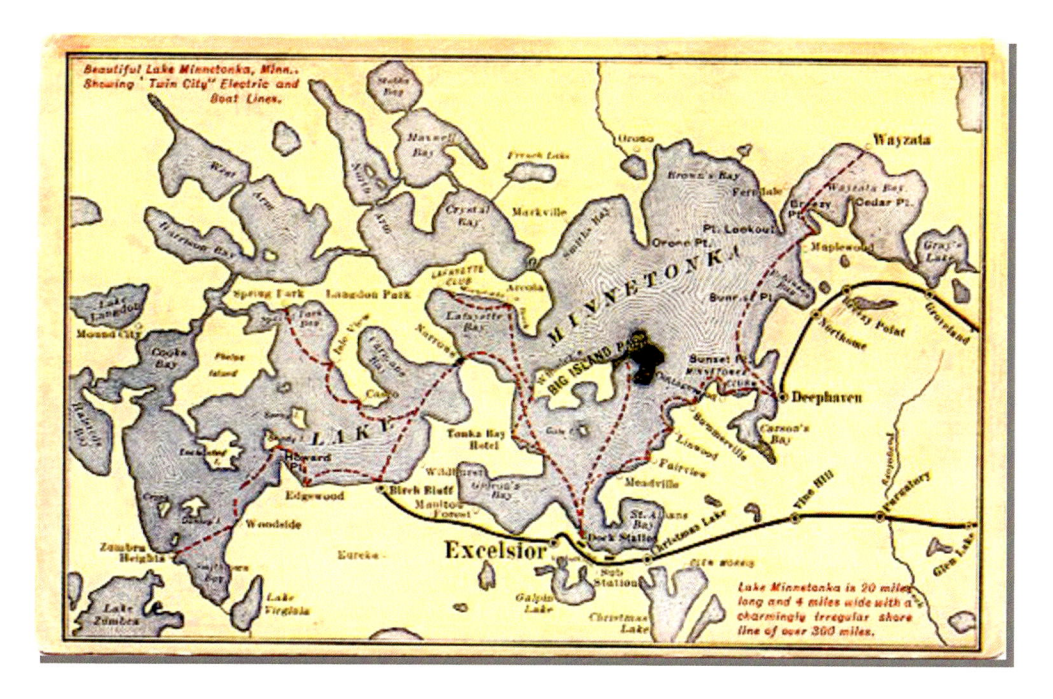

This postcard map from the early 1900's shows the unique configuration of Lake Minnetonka with its many bays, channels, islands and points.

Lake Minnetonka is not a single lake, but is rather an unusual combination of three of the four known types of lakes in the world. This unusual configuration helps to explain the variety of aquatic plants and numerous fish species that inhabit the lake. With its close proximity to the highly populated Twin Cities area it is one of the greatest recreational lakes in all America.

PREFACE

Lake Minnetonka has a unique history, especially its early history, the incredible 1880's, the 1890's, the exciting Roaring Twenties with its flappers, straw hats, spats, the Charleston, automobiles, wool swimming suits, row boats and much more.

I captured some of this in my book, "Picturing Lake Minnetonka," published by the Minnesota Historical Society in 2001. While researching for this first book, I learned a great deal about the lake and its historic past. I also learned that to keep history and legends alive, their stories must be told and retold. I felt that there was a further need to share additional information and documentation that I had acquired.

Over the next few years I created ten historical documents which I call "Insights." Each one is a stand alone, colored eight page publication on a specific subject, (steamboats, hotels, etc.) With each one, I included some common lake history.

Several people have suggested that I combine all ten "Insights" into one book.. This book is that combination! It results in an informative, overlapping, sometimes repetitive collection of historic documentation. I hope that you will enjoy it as much as I have had writing it.

Jim Ogland

EARLY HISTORY

LAKE MINNETONKA

When French explorers came to Minnesota in the seventeenth century, they encountered two major Indian nations: the Dakota or Sioux, and the Chippewa or Ojibway. The principle inhabitants of Lake Minnetonka were the "Mighty Dakotah." They lived primarily in the river valleys, but came to Lake Minnetonka for ceremonies, celebrations and games. Located in the heart of the *"Big Woods,"* Minnetonka was rich in wild rice, berries, roots, and fruit. There was an abundance of fish, game and waterfowl. The Indians loved to hunt and fish here. Over four hundred Indian burial mounds were discovered around the lake. Until the Indian uprising conflict in 1862, several bands lived peacefully on the shores. By 1870 all of the Indians had moved on.

COMING OF THE WHITE MAN

The first discovery of the lake by the white man came in May of 1822, when two young boys, one a drummer boy, from nearby Fort Snelling, paddled their canoe up Minnehaha Creek. Their discovery went un-noticed until 1852, when treaties with the Indians were signed, and the area was opened up for settlement. Pioneers, anxious to stake a claim, began pouring into the region. Villages soon developed around the lake at Wayzata, Excelsior and Mound City.

THE GLORY YEARS AT LAKE MINNETONKA

Stories of beautiful Minnetonka spread widely during the Civil War, and at its conclusion in 1865, visitors from the deep South began arriving. They had heard about the cool summers and the healthful atmosphere. They came by steamboats up the Mississippi, and then by the railroad that would soon reach Wayzata on the northern shore. Encouraged by the large numbers of visitors, hotels, boarding houses and inns sprang up along the shores, each trying to outdo the other. By 1876, over 6000 guests reportedly were registered at five hotels. The first of several large hotels, the "Hotel St. Louis," opened at Deephaven in 1879. It was closely followed the same year by the huge "Lake Park Hotel" at Tonka Bay. Soon James J. Hill, the "Empire Builder," completed his gigantic "Hotel Lafayette" at Minnetonka Beach. Opening on the Fourth of July, 1882, it was said to be the biggest and best hotel West of New York City. Hill also built the enormous 300ft steamboat, *"Belle of Minnetonka,"* to compete with the 160ft *"City of St. Louis."* Before it was over, there would be some ninety steamboats on the lake. The 1880s were clearly the *"Glory Years,"* but by 1893 the tourists from the south were going elsewhere. Minnetonka's great resort days were over!

THE STREETCAR / STEAMBOATS

In the summer of 1905, streetcars began rolling westward to Excelsior and Lake Minnetonka. With them came excited tourists and first time visitors looking for summer fun. All but forgotten as a tourist attraction, Minnetonka was set to come alive again. Thomas Lowry and the Twin City Rapid Transit Company were building an amusement park on Big Island and developing a fleet of six fast *Streetcar/Steamboats*. Painted yellow like their streetcar cousins, they were cute and jaunty. Routes were established to carry passengers to anywhere on the lake. A whole new era was unfolding at Lake Minnetonka. The *"Golden Years"* had arrived.

Lake Minnetonka

Historical Insights

The following Ten *"Insights"* are a collection of informative records of early Lake Minnetonka history

Lake Minnetonka
Incredible Hotels
Huge Steamboats
Historic Excelsior
Wayzata
Yachting
Mound
Big Island
Minnehaha
Postcards

By Jim Ogland, author of "Picturing Lake Minnetonka"

DNALGO Enterprises Box 935 Wayzata, Mn 55391

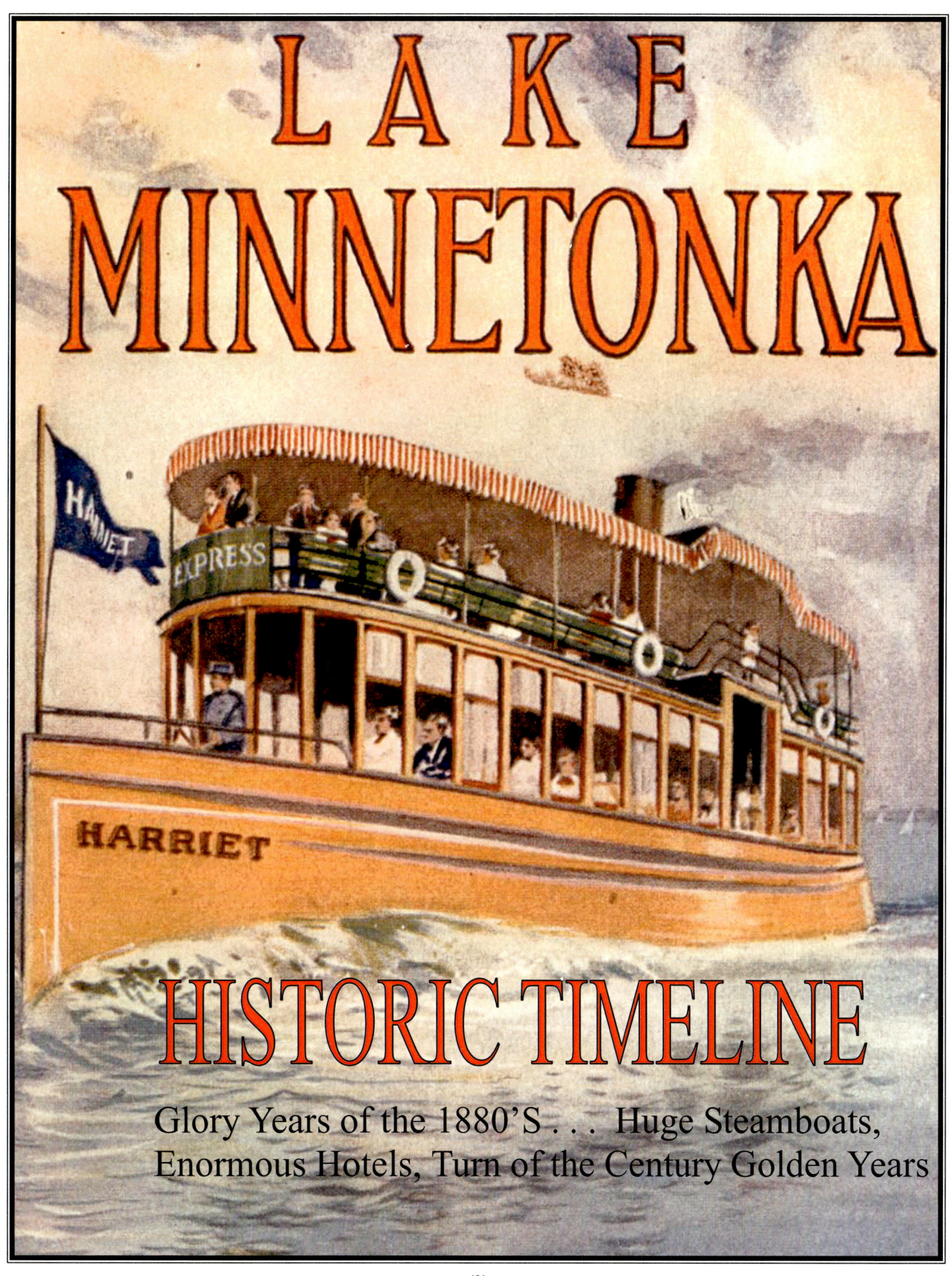

LAKE MINNETONKA

HISTORIC TIMELINE

Glory Years of the 1880'S . . . Huge Steamboats, Enormous Hotels, Turn of the Century Golden Years

LAKE MINNETONKA TIME LINE

A chronological record of Lake Minnetonka's early history

1670s French trappers refer to Minnetonka as *"lac gros"* in the *"grand bois,"* "Big lake in the woods."

1819 Fort Snelling is established as northwesternmost army post on the U.S. frontier.

1822 Fort Snelling teens, Joe Brown & Will Snelling paddle up Minnehaha Creek and *discover* Lake Minnetonka.

1851 Important "Traverse de Sioux and Mendota Treaties" are **signed with Indians,** opening way for pioneer settlement.

1852 Simon Stevens and Calvin Tuttle re-discover Lake Minnetonka, build dam and sawmill at Minnetonka Mills. Governor Alexander Ramsey visits lake. After learning that Indians call it "Min-ni-tan-ka," he officially names it Minnetonka.

1853 First hotel in lake area opened, located at Minnetonka Mills. Pioneer Association headed by George Bertram arrives from New York and **settled Excelsior.**

1854 The "Pre-emption Privilege Act" is extended to Minnesota Territory. Allows settlers to stake a claim. **Village of Wayzata is laid out** by Oscar Garrison and Alfred Robinson. Cook House built in Mound.

1855 "Song of Hiawatha" is published by Longfellow. Puts Minnehaha Falls and Minnesota on the map. **First stagecoach began operation** from Wayzata to St. Anthony and St. Paul, operated three times weekly. Cholera breaks out in Wayzata. First death is recorded.

1857 Ginseng plants found growing wild. Digging the sought-after medicinal roots brings quick money to many.

1858 Minnesota admitted to the Union. **Becomes the 32th state** on May 11, 1858.

1860 Rev. Charles Galpin of Excelsior **builds first steamboat,** named the *"Governor Ramsey."* Abraham Lincoln elected president.

1862 Indian uprising at New Ulm panics local settlers; many head for safety at Fort Snelling. Others board boats to Big Island.

1867 Railroad comes to Minnetonka. First train arrives at Wayzata on the 25th of July.

1868 First propeller steamboat, the *"Sue Gardiner,"* launched by Charles Gardiner.

1869 Following the Civil War, **visitors begin arriving** from the deep south. Area seen as healthy, cool nights, and beautiful.

1876 Editor A.S. Dimond begins publication of *Lake Minnetonka Tourist.* **Chapman House opens in Mound on 4th of July.**

1879 Sir Charles Gibson opens Hotel St. Louis in Deephaven. **First major hotel** on the lake, has 200 rooms. Huge Lake Park Hotel at Tonka Bay is also completed and opened. (shown below)

1881 1000 passenger, 160ft. *"City of St. Louis"* **steamboat,** owned by W. D. Washburn, launched at Wayzata on June 4th.

1882 Not to be outdone, James J. Hill builds enormous Hotel Layfayette at Minnetonka Beach, also commissions the *"Belle of Minnetonka."* The **300 foot long, 2500 passenger steamboat dwarfs all others.** Great rivalry develops with the *City of St.Louis.* Minnetonka Yacht Club is organized. George A. Brackett becomes the first Commodore.

1883 *Glory Years* at Minnetonka are here. Hundreds of visitors arrive weekly. **10,000 guests were registered** in the three major hotels during June & July.

1885 With his railroad tracks now reaching Spring Park, J.J. Hill opens Hotel Del Otero, one of the largest on the lake. It will survive for the next sixty years. Keewaydin Hotel also opens in Cottagewood.

1892 Heyday of the big steamboats is drawing to a close. The *"Belle of Minnetonka"* remains tied to the dock all summer.

1893 James J. Hill feuds with Wayzata about location of tracks on lakeshore. In spite, he relocates depot to the edge of town. **An incredible new sailboat, the *"Onawa,"* is designed and built in Deephaven by Arthur Dyer for the Burton family.** The *"Onawa"* sweeps every race in which it is entered.

1897 Hotel Lafayette destroyed by fire. The *Glory Years* are ending. One by one, the fabulous hotels & huge steamboats are disappearing. **Guests from the South and East are going elsewhere,** to Yellowstone, Mackinac Island, etc.

1904 Excelsior Casino opens on the shore at the foot of Water St. Features a bowling alley, restaurant and a roller skating rink.

1905 *Golden Years arrive.* Excelsior residents **awake to the rumble of streetcars** on Water Street. Thomas Lowry's Twin City Rapid Transit Company is about to forever change Lake Minnetonka.

1906 Six unique, **fast Express Boats** resembling their yellow streetcar cousins, are launched in Excelsior, and begin a new shuttle service to anywhere on the lake. TCRT also opens a **Picnic and Amusement Park** on Big Island. *Minnetonka once more comes alive.*

J. J. Hill relents and constructs new train depot at Wayzata. Said to be the finest on the line.

1911 First bridge spans the Narrows, replacing a hand operated ferry. President Wm Howard Taft tours the lake and makes Lafayette Club his summer White House. **TCRT abruptly closes Big Island** operations at end of season. Ferry, excursion boats and island structures are dismantled.

1925 Excelsior Amusement Park opens. Has a roller coaster, merry-go-round, ferris wheel, a fun house and other attractions.

1926 Ridership has fallen off sharply. Streetcar boat operations are suspended. **Three boats, including the *Minnehaha*, are sunk in deep water** off Big Island.

1945 Hotel Del Otero burns on July 16th. **Last of the big hotels,** the end of an era.

1973 Excelsior **Amusement Park closes** on Labor Day, September 3, following forty nine seasons of operation.

1990 After fifty-four years on the bottom of the lake, a six year restoration begins on the recovered 70ft steamboat, *Minnehaha*. On May 25, 1996, the *Minnehaha* **celebrates it's Maiden Voyage** and once again is returned to passenger service on the lake.

2000 The 19th and 20th centuries were unquestionably the most unique and fascinating periods in Lake Minnetonka history. There were huge hotels, steamboats and good times.

(4)

EARLY HISTORY

When French explorers came to Minnesota in the seventeenth century, they encountered two major Indian nations: the Dakota or Sioux, and the Chippewa or Ojibway. The principle inhabitants of Lake Minnetonka were the "Mighty Dakcotah." They lived primarily in the river valleys, but came to Lake Minnetonka for ceremonies, celebrations and games. Located in the heart of the "Big Woods," Minnetonka was rich in wild rice, berries, and fruit. There was an abundance of fish, game and waterfowl. The Indians loved to hunt and fish here. Over four hundred Indian burial mounds were discovered around the lake. Until the Indian uprising conflict in 1862, several bands lived peacefully on the shores. By 1870 all of the Indians had moved on.

DISCOVERY

Lake Minnetonka is located in central Minnesota and is just west of the Twin Cities of Minneapolis and St. Paul. It was a favorite place of the early American Indians. They called it "mi-ni-tan-ka," *a great place of water or big water.* In 1822 two young boys from nearby Fort Snelling decided to go exploring. **They began their outing at a beautiful waterfall, later named Minnehaha Falls.** Canoeing up the stream that supplied the falls, they soon discovered that it went farther than anyone had previously realized. After paddling most of the day along its twisting, turning and meandering path through dense woods and over sparse prairie grass, *they made an astonishing discovery.* The little creek that they had been following flowed from the most beautiful lake that anyone could imagine. It was a deep blue, and the breeze blowing across it was cool and refreshing. The sun glinted and sparkled on every wave. There were islands, peninsulas and many bays; large and small, all connected to each other. It was an unexpected, awesome sight. **It was the discovery of Lake Minnetonka.**

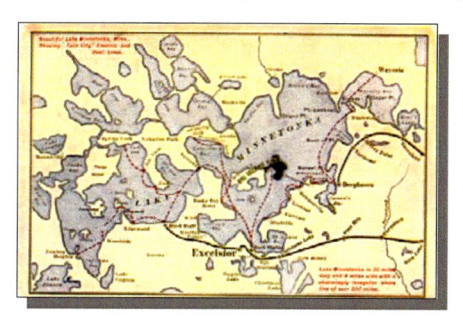

Their discovery went unnoticed until 1852, when treaties with the Indians were signed, and the area was opened up for development. Pioneers, anxious to stake a claim, began pouring into the region. Villages soon developed around the lake at Wayzata, Excelsior, Mound, Deephaven and Tonka Bay.

Lake Minnetonka is not a single lake, but rather an unusual combination of three of the four known types of lakes in the world. This unusual configuration helps to explain the variety of aquatic plants and numerous fish species that inhabit the lake. With its close proximity to the highly populated Twin Cities area, it is one of the greatest recreational lakes in all America.

PIONEERS

Within a few years, pioneers and early settlers began arriving. The settlers could homestead 160 acres if they built a log cabin and stayed for a year. *Small communities gradually sprang up around the lake.* Excelsior was settled in 1853, Wayzata in 1854. Big Island was homesteaded by Wm Morse in 1856. The area's soil was rich and fertile and as a result numerous vineyards, orchards and farms prospered along the shores. Later on, a fruit growers association was formed in Excelsior, and the area became well known for its abundance of fine fruit and vegetables. Friendly Sioux Indians still inhabited the area and continued to hunt the plentiful game and gather the wild rice that grew abundantly on the lake's shoreline. Chief Shakopee and his band camped near Wayzata until the Sioux outbreak in 1862. The name Wayzata came from the Sioux word meaning "North Shore" or the *Northern God, a fabled giant who lives in the North and blows cold out of his mouth."*

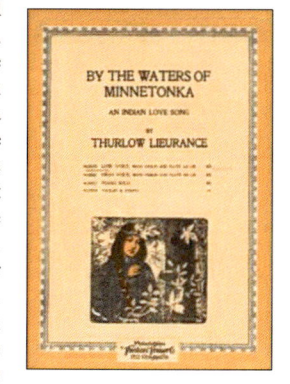

THE GLORY YEARS

Stories of beautiful Minnetonka spread widely during the Civil War, and at its conclusion in 1865, visitors from the deep south began arriving. They had heard about the cool summers and the healthful atmosphere. They came by steamboat up the Mississippi, and then by the railroad that would soon reach Wayzata on the northern shore. Encouraged by the large numbers of visitors, hotels, boarding houses and inns sprang up around the lake, each trying to outdo the other. By 1876, over 6000 guests reportedly were registered at five hotels. The first of several large hotels, the "Hotel St. Louis," opened at Deephaven in 1879. It was closely followed the same year by the huge "Lake Park Hotel" at Tonka Bay. Soon James J. Hill, the "Empire Builder," completed his gigantic "Hotel Lafayette" at Minnetonka Beach. Opening on the Fourth of July 1882, it was said to be the biggest and best hotel West of New York City. Lake Minnetonka was fast becoming a major resort area.

HUGE STEAMBOATS

The first steamboat arrived at the Wayzata docks in the year 1860. It was built by a ship's carpenter for the Reverend Charles Galpin of Excelsior and was named the *"Governor Ramsey."* The flat bottom, fifty foot side-wheeler was the beginning of the incredible era of steamboats, railroads and large hotels. After a few years, the race was on to see who could build the biggest, the fastest, the most luxurious steamboat. *Before it was over, there would be more than ninety.* The incredible steamboat era reached its zenith in 1881 when the "City of St. Louis" was constructed at Wayzata by W.D. Washburn who had a financial interest in the St. Louis Hotel. It was one hundred and sixty feet long, forty feet wide, and carried over one thousand passengers. Not to be outdone, James J. Hill, builder of the enormous Lafayette Hotel, launched the *"Belle of Minnetonka."* With a length of 300 feet and beam of sixty, it was the largest boat ever built at Lake Minnetonka. It had a capacity for twenty five hundred passengers. An intense rivalry developed between the two boats. After meeting the trains in Wayzata they would square off and race across the seven miles of open water to Excelsior. With smoke billowing from their stacks and with their engines pounding, they were off to Minnetonka Beach and the upper lake. **The Glory Years had arrived! It was the dawn of an exciting, wonderful, and marvelous era. Lake Minnetonka would never again be the same.** Countless thousands of tourists and visitors would ride the magnificent steamboats before it was over. To see the boats lined up at the Wayzata docks awaiting the trains, blowing their whistles in anticipation, was a sight to behold. Families from the South arrived with what seemed like endless quantities of luggage and servants. They came for the summer and they came for a good time.

The large hotels competed with each other for business and their steamboats were an important part of their overall image. More importantly, they provided transportation to and from the railroad stations for the increasing number of visitors and vacationers.

THE RAILROADS

In 1867, the St Paul and Pacific Railway extended its line to Lake Minnetonka at Wayzata; thus it became the first railroad to the lake. Others soon followed, including the *Minneapolis and St. Louis Railway* on the south shore, providing service to Deephaven, Excelsior and Tonka Bay. The *Chicago Milwaukee Railway* to Bay St. Louis, and eventually the *Great Northern Railway* on the north shore provided service to Wayzata, Minnetonka Beach, Spring Park and Mound. *After the end of the Civil War, thousand of visitors from the South began vacationing in the area.* They came from near and far, and the railroads which promoted Lake Minnetonka as a resort area, were only too eager to bring them. In the summer of 1883, over 10,000 guests registered at the three major hotels and an estimated 2,500 excursionists

(5)

visited the lake each day. The trip from Minneapolis to Wayzata took about twenty five minutes, and the time to Excelsior was just under an hour. Guests came not only for recreation, but came to escape the intense heat and humidity of the summer south. In addition to its sheer beauty, the area was also well known as a health resort. Its cool nights, refreshing breezes, and moderate temperatures were deemed helpful for those with consumption. This was the *Iron Rail Era* and it played an important part in the development of Lake Minnetonka.

INCREDIBLE HOTELS

First of the big hotels was the magnificent summer resort, *Hotel St. Louis*. It opened in 1879 at Deephaven with a capacity for over four hundred guests. It was a major attraction for tourists from New Orleans, St. Louis, and Kansas City. Constructed the same year was the lavish *Lake Park Hotel* at Tonka Bay, (later re-named the Tonka Bay Hotel). It had rooms for over 1000 guests and its dining room could seat 400 persons and reportedly served the best cuisine to be found in the area. It was a huge complex that included a casino with a large roller skating rink. In addition to these major hotels, there were smaller hotels and cottages scattered around the lake. Some of the more prominent included the Arlington House in Wayzata, the Sampson House, White House and Hotel LaPaul in Excelsior, and the Palmer House at Zumbra Heights. **In Deephaven, the Cottagewood Hotel, later named the Hotel Keewaydin, provided a quiet restful time.** The Hotel Del Otero in Spring Park was a spacious three story hotel that featured a casino and dancing pavilion and vast picnic grounds. The Maple Heights Inn, better known as Woolnoughs, and even later as Tippiwauken, was located nearby on Island Park. At Mound and the upper lake, several poplur hotels provided memorable accommodations and numerous additional services, rental boats, etc. They were the well known Chapman House, Bartletts, the Dewey House, and the Hotel Buena Vista. There were other hotels on Shady Island, Crane, and Enchanted Islands, as well as the Edgewood at Birch Bluff. The smaller ones were perhaps more restful.

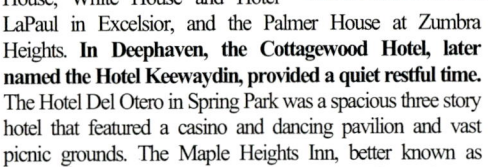

The largest and plushest of all the hotels was the gigantic *"Lafayette Hotel"* constructed in 1882 by James J. Hill's Great Northern Railroad at Minnetonka Beach. It was five stories high, 745 feet long and had approximately 300 rooms.

THE GOLDEN YEARS

The 1880's were clearly the "Glory Years," but by 1893 the tourists from the South were going elsewhere. The same railroads that had brought them here were taking them to Yellowstone Park, to Mackinac Island and the Seaside Resorts of the East coast. **Minnetonka's great resort days were over!**

The lake had been more or less forgotten as a tourist attraction, then suddenly in 1905 Thomas Lowry and his Twin City Rapid Transit Company began to change all that. Embarking on an incredibly ambitious plan, Lowry purchased the huge Tonka Bay hotel, bought sixty five acres on Big Island, (on which to build an amusement park), ordered the construction of six fast streetcar-like Express Boats, extended his streetcar line to Excelsior and Deephaven, and purchased all the remaining excursion and passenger steamboats on the lake. He further commissioned construction of three 142 foot, one thousand passenger ferry boats, all of this to be completed and ready for the 1907 summer season. It was an enormous undertaking! **The Amusement Park in itself was a major project.** It was a natural spot for an amusement and picnic park in a spectacular, strategic location, only a few miles off shore on Big Island, within a twenty minute ferry ride from the Excelsior docks. **The Glory Years at Lake Minnetonka were gone. The wealthy Southerners were vacationing elsewhere. In their place were local excursionists and a new kind of tourist, a tourist that would come to the lake just for the day.** The new tourists came, and they came by the thousands! They were encouraged by the Twin City Rapid Transit Company's new streetcar line from Minneapolis / St. Paul to Excelsior and James J. Hill's new Great Northern Depot in Wayzata. They came to ride the new excursion and express boats. They came to picnic or board a ferryboat for the two mile ride to the new amusement park at Big Island. The three, one-thousand passenger capacity ferryboats often carried as many as 15,000 passengers on a single Sunday or holiday.

THE AMUSEMENT PARK

A.W. Warnock, General Passenger Agent of the Twin City Rapid Transit Company wrote: *It is the most beautiful park in all the Northwest. It has unexcelled facilities to entertain Lodge, Club, Sunday School or Society picnics of any kind. Kitchens, toilet rooms, shelter houses, water supplies, all include the best and latest improvements for comfort and convenience.* All the structures on the island were of the *Spanish mission style architecture* and were exceedingly attractive. Probably the most novel was the *peristyle,* following the ridge of the island. It was built of concrete and outlined with electric lights. The two hundred foot tower was also built of steel and concrete, and was perhaps the most unusual structure on the island, in that it was a close copy of the famous tower of Seville, Spain. It contained the island's water supply, and at night was beautifully illuminated with hundreds of lights, and like a beacon, it could be seen from all parts of the lake. The park's main attraction, however, was the *music casino,* built of steel, concrete and glass. It could seat 1500 persons comfortably. **Perhaps the most famous band to play at the casino was the popular John Phillip Sousa orchestra.** The park also had several popular amusement rides including a figure eight roller coaster, a penny arcade, an old mill ride and a ride through Yellowstone Park.

STREETCAR BOATS

Six fast torpedo stern Express Boats were built at the company shops at 31st and Nicollet and launched in April and May of 1906. Like their streetcar cousins they were painted bright yellow and quickly became the darlings of the lake. They operated for over twenty years and provided needed transportation to all points of the lake.

In the early summer of 1905, streetcars began rolling westward to Excelsior and Lake Minnetonka. A new era of transportation had arrived. As many as sixty streetcars were sometimes on the line at the same time. Fast Express Boats on regular scheduled runs also whisked residents to and from their cottages.

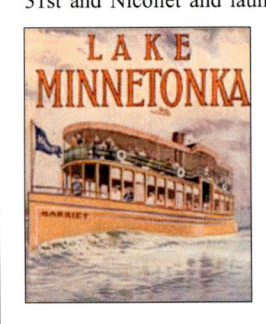

PARK CLOSES

By 1911 attendance had dropped off sharply and at the end of the summer season the park was abruptly closed The Tonka Bay Hotel was also closed and all operations ceased, including the ferry and excursion boats. Only the Streetcar Boats continued to operate and even their schedules were reduced. **Other changes were also occurring,** though this was still the horse and buggy days, the automobile was just around the corner. Cottages were springing up, spreading out from the main towns of Mound, Wayzata, and Excelsior. Residents of the Twin Cities were not vacationing at the big hotels. They were building or buying cottages!

BIG ISLAND

Big Island was a favorite place of the early American Indians. They hunted, fished, fought many battles, and held important ceremonies on the island. It was the site of numerous Indian legends and myths. The island had many large sugar maple trees from which their annual sugar supply was obtained. They called the island **"Wetutonka"** which meant, "the spring move to the sugar camp." The island also became known as **"Cottage Island"** because of the unusual Indian houses found there. They were built of logs and skins, not at all like the traditional Sioux Indian teepee.

1822 Young teens from Fort Snelling, Will Snelling and Joe Brown, paddle up Minnehaha Creek to the lakes outlet at Grays Bay. They spent the first night camped on **Big Island** becoming the first white men to discover Lake Minnetonka and Big Island. Colonel Snelling was not pleased about their escapade and forbid discussion of their discovery. It did not appear on any area maps. The Indians kept its location a secret. Thirty years go by before next visit by any white men.

1852 On April 8th, **Simon Stevens and Calvin Tuttle re-discover** Lake Minnetonka and like the earlier teens, **camp their first night on Big Island.** The lake is still frozen and covered with thick ice. They hike and explore most of the lake. A month later in May, **Governor Ramsey** visits the lake with a party led by Stevens. He names the lake *Minnetonka* after the Indian name Minne-tanka. In August of 1852, **Mrs Elizabeth Ellet,** a well known New York writer, visits the lake and describes Big Island in her book, *"Summer Rambles in the West."* She is one of the first white women to explore Minnetonka. On September 6, 1852, another party of eminent men visit the lake and name the island *Owens Island* after a member of their party, Col. John P. Owens. Later, on September 18th, Judge Bradley B. Meeker, stakes a claim on the island and it becomes known as **Meeker Island.**

Amusement Park 200' Tower

Big Island is the largest of the lakes several islands not connected by a bridge. It is actually made up of three islands which in total contain 275 acres. A channel divides the two largest areas and a separate small area on the north side is called Mahpiyata Island, named after a beautiful Indian maiden.

1854 W.B. Morse, with his brother John, acquired the island. **He sub-divided it and developed lots.** The island then became known as **Morse Island** and finally as **Big Island**. Prominent points on the southside of the island are named *Point Charming, Point Comfort and Crown Point.*

1862 During the Indian uprising, a large boatload of settlers headed for the safety of Big Island. They had engine trouble and did not make it to the island, but managed to survive.

1891 Olaf Searle, a wealthy Norwegian immigrant, purchased 125 acres and built a magnificent three story twenty-one room mansion on the north side of the island. It is the first home on the lake to have steam heat and gas lights. He had a channel dug separating the two large land areas, and also built a foot bridge to Mahpiyata Island.

1906 The **Twin City Rapid Transit Company** decided to expand their operation to Minnetonka and began construction of a **65 acre picnic and amusement park** on the island. (see *"Golden Years"* for detailed description of the park).

1911 At the end of the 1911 season, the **amusement park closed for good.** The buildings and peristyle walls that encircled the park were torn down and removed. It was the end of a brief, but exciting period.

Foot bridge to Mahpiyata Island

1916 The 65 acre park site was sold to several veterans' organizations. It was to be used as a camp ground and recreational location for World War I veterans and their families. The camp is still in operation to this day.

1971 The United States Power Squadron, a boating educational organization, acquired several acres and developed a members' rendezvous location.

Hennepin County Parks has also received numerous acres on the north side as gifts from various land owners. Over the years a number of seasonal recreational cabins have been built throughout the island. The north shore of the island is a popular gathering spot for boaters to raft together.

THE YACHT CLUBS

Yachting on the lake became a serious pursuit in 1882 with the formation of the Minnetonka Yacht Club. The *Glory Years of the 1880's* were just getting underway when James J. Hill, the railroad magnate, built the massive, opulent, Hotel Lafayette at Minnetonka Beach. As part of the inaugural opening weekend on the Fourth of July, 1882, a somewhat loosely organized sailboat race was held on the lake. Later in the summer the men who had raced that day met to form the *Minnetonka Yacht Club.*

Almost from its beginning, the new club held weekly regattas with as many as twenty boats at the starting line. George A. Brackett was elected its first commodore. Brackett was among the lake's first "cottagers," and he, with some of his fellow summer residents, formed a yacht club that today is one of the oldest in America.

In 1889 the two clubs merged. With their larger combined membership, they decided to build new docks and a clubhouse somewhere on the lake. Sir Charles Gibson of the St. Louis Hotel offered the club $3000 and a small manmade island, named Lighthouse Island, at the entrance to Carson's Bay. The new clubhouse, designed by Harry Wild Jones, survived for over fifty years until finally burning down in 1943.

1883 Another club was formed; the Excelsior Yacht Club. Competition between the two clubs was stiff and crews demanded much from their boats. Most boats were built in New England by well-known designers such as the Herreshoff Brothers. But soon, local builders began turning out boats that were equal to, if not better than, those being purchased in the East. The boats were large and fast with plenty of sail area. They were gaff-rigged, often with up to 1000 feet of sail, and were called *"sandbaggers"* because of the sand they carried for ballast.

1890 The first championship regatta of the season was held July 1, 1890. The big event, however, was the formal opening of the new clubhouse on July 18th. The picturesque structure would become a Minnetonka landmark for the next half century. A navy blue double-breasted sack cloth coat and pants of the best quality was approved as the club's uniform. Caps would be white and the club flag, white with a blue star and a red edge.

1892 Newly adopted rules made possible a radical change in the design of inland sailboats. The following year, Hazen Burton and his son, Ward, of Deephaven, commissioned Arthur Dyer to build a new design. The result was the famous *Onawa*. During its racing life, the *Onawa* swept every race it entered, including east coast regattas.

1899 Hard water sailing: The Minnetonka Ice Club was incorporated with Theodore Wetmore serving as its first Commodore. Within two years the club had 167 members and 17 boats. Some boats came from the Hudson River and were up to sixty feet in length. *Northern Light* and *Zero*, owned by Ward Burton, set new speed records. Wetmore donated a three story house on Bug Island to be used for the Ice Yacht Clubhouse. It was destroyed by fire on January 14, 1904.

1893 The newly designed boats used the principle of sailing over, rather than through the water. They sailed without ballast and were more easily handled than previous designs. **These changes eventually led to the current racing scow design.**

1904 A third Yacht Club was formed at Excelsior as the Minnetonka Boat Club. A younger element in the club felt the Minnetonka Club was becoming to exclusive. Eventually differences were reconciled and in 1907 they rejoined the Minnetonka Yacht Club.

1943 Disaster: On August 31st, the clubhouse with its unique witches peaks caught fire, fanned by high winds was completely destroyed. Also lost were trophies, rare photographs, flags and banners. It was a tragic loss!

1944 Almost immediately a committee began planning the construction of a new clubhouse. With WWII on, immediate rebuilding would have to wait, but on August 2, the cornerstone was laid for the new clubhouse.

GLOSSARY OF LAKE MINNETONKA PLACE NAMES

Most Lake Minnetonka place names come from one of three general categories: (1) early settlers or landowners (Stubbs, Swift, Carman), (2) characteristics of the richly endowed natural environment (Birch Bluff, Maplewoods, Deephaven), or (3) the native American Sioux Indian (Wayzata, Spirit Knob, Wawatasso), etc.

ARLINGTON HEIGHTS — area just east of Wayzata on the lakeshore between the railroad tracks and lake. In 1878 the site of a hotel by that name.
ARCOLA — name given by the Great Northern to a passenger stop just across the Crystal Bay bridge approaching Minnetonka Beach. Earlier called Northwood.
BIG WOODS or **BOIS GRAND** — Minnetonka area often included in the great tract of deciduous forest known to early settlers as the Big Woods.
BIG ISLAND — first called Meeker's Island for Judge Bradley B. Meeker, who settled there in 1852. In 1854 W. B. Morse purchased it. Called Morse Island.
BIRCH BLUFF — a reference to the birch trees along the high bluff on the south shore of the upper lake.
BOHNS POINT — north shore of Crystal Bay, named for Gebhard C. Bohn of St. Paul. Purchased in 1883.
BRACKETTS POINT — named for George A. Brackett who purchased the point in 1880, named it Orono after his home in Maine. Earlier called Starvation Point.
BREEZY POINT — on the south side of the entrance to Wayzata Bay, part of Maplewoods. Spirit Knob once marked the end of the point.
BROWNS BAY — in the lower lake, named for James B. Brown, an early settler from Kentucky, who built a log cabin on that shore line.
BUSHAWAY — north shore of Grays Bay on Hwy101. An English corruption of Bourgeois. George and Lewis Bourgeois took up a claim in this area in 1852-53.
CARMANS BAY — named for John Carman, first white settler to establish residence in Orono Township. Settled in Spring Park area in 1853. He had a brother Frank.
CARSONS BAY — named for Elijah Carson, brother of famous Kit Carson, who settled in the area in the early 1850's.
CASCO POINT — between Spring Park Bay and Carmans Bay. May have been named by a settler from Casco Bay, Maine — a great summer resort.
CEDAR POINT — name came from abundance of cedar trees in area. Part of Maplewoods. Also a Cedar Point in upper lake.
CEDARHURST — Russell M. Bennett, so named his estate in Deephaven about 1900 on land purchased from Sir Charles Gibson.
COOKS BAY — on the upper lake named for Matthew S. Cook — land owner and resort operator in 1876.
COTTAGEWOOD — south shore of lower lake between Carsons Bay and Cottagewood Bay. Hit by tornado in 1965.
CRANE ISLAND — once the home of blue herons, mistakenly called cranes.
CRYSTAL BAY — named because of the unusually crystalline transparency of the water. So named by Allen French, A Quaker from North Carolina.
DEEPHAVEN — a haven deep in the woods. Now a city. It was named by Mrs. Hazen Burton.
DEERING ISLAND — named for Charles W. Deering who headquartered his propeller driven boat, the Florence M. Deering, in West Arm in the 1880's.
EAGLE ISLAND — upper lake, home of eagles in early days.
EAGLE BLUFF — on left at entrance in Halsted's Bay.
ENCHANTED ISLAND — named by white settlers and refers to Indian ceremonials and medicine dances in pre-settler days.
EXCELSIOR — the motto of New York State, from which George Bertram and Company's first settlers came, means "ever upward." Area also called vinelands because the region produced such fine grapes.
FERGUSONS POINT — named for William H. Ferguson, first settler on the point and a fruit grower. Lower lake, south side, sometimes called Gluek's Point.
FERNDALE — named by James J. Hill, to identify spot on his railroad in an area overgrown with ferns, where area businessmen might board his train. This was at the time Hill had moved the Wayzata station to Holdridge in the 1890's.
FRENCH LAKE — named for the French family who were Quakers from Ohio.
GALES ISLAND — lower lake, south of Big Island. Named for Harlow Gale who purchased the island in 1872. First called Gooseberry Island, and then Brightwood. At $2.50 an acre, Mr Gale paid less than $4.00 for the island.
GIBSON POINT — part of Northome entering Robinson Bay. Named for Sir Charles Gibson of St. Louis, who owned 200 acres in the area.
GLUEKS POINT — named for brothers John, Louis and Charles Gluek. Point earlier called Fergusons Point, on south shore in Cottagewood.
GRANDVIEW POINT — entrance to Carsons Bay on Cottagewood side. Earlier called Donaldsons Point and broken up into half acre lots in the 1970's.
GRAYS BAY — named for Amos N. Gray, a carpenter, and brother-in-law of Joseph and Wm Chowen. All took pre-emption claims around Mtka in 1852.
GREENWOOD — classed as a city on the south shore, lower lake between Deephaven and Excelsior.

HALSTEDS BAY — upper lake, corruption of the family name of Frank Halstead who came in 1855 from New Jersey and drowned in 1876, and his brother George who came soon after, and died in 1901.
HARDSCRABBLE POINT — in southeast corner of Cooks Bay, named in honor of an early English settler.
HARRISONS BAY — towards northwest corner of lake area. Named for ship builder, Capt. N.S. Harrison, who owned a farm on the north shoreline with immense wild rice fields in 1875.
HERMITAGE — upper lake, opposite Crane Island. Home of the Halstead brothers. They are buried there on former site of Loring Woodend Farms.
HOLDRIDGE — named for Mrs. Charles Babcock, the former Florence Holdridge. Important in the 1890s, when James J. Hill moved the Wayzata Station east a mile, to show his pique at being sued by the Wayzata citizenry, not far from where #101 crosses the railroad tracks in Wayzata.
HOWARDS POINT — upper lake, named for M. S. Howard pioneer family.
HULLS NARROWS — named for Rev. Stephen Hull, the first settler on the upper lake. In 1851 he settled on the strait (a 40-acre marsh full of wild rice) between the upper and lower lake. He enlarged Crystal Creek in 1873 to provide steamboat passage from upper to lower lake.
HUNTINGTON POINT — named for W.W. Huntington of Arcola. Earlier called Holmes Point, until 1874.
JENNINGS BAY — named for F.A. Jennings, a printer who made a clearing in the West end of West Arm.
KEEWAYDIN — an early hotel in Cottagewood. Named from Longfellow's Song of Hiawatha, and means Northwest Wind.
LAFAYETTE BAY — named after James J. Hill's luxurious hotel of that name, near the present site of the Layfayette Club.
LOCKES POINT — W. H. Locke of Cincinnati was the second owner. First owner was William Lithgow of Boston who drowned in 1854. The area was a battleground between the Sioux and Chippewas. Now know as Clay Cliff and the Crawford Johnson estate. Mrs. Johnson was the daughter of Fred B. Synder, long time owner of Clay Cliff, located in Tonka Bay.
LOOKOUT POINT — part of todays Ferndale. A buoy off this point is known to all lake sailors. First called Blithwood in 1883, and then Harringtons Point.
MAHPIYATA ISLAND (May-pi-ya-ta) — Sioux "Celestial Peace Maiden," a Dakota legend. Island on NE corner of channel running thru Big Island. Once part of Olaf Searle's estate.
MAPLEWOOD — the maples are still there. A lovely area across Wayzata Bay on south shore.
MAXWELL BAY — named for John Maxwell, an old soldier in Wellington's army who settled there, north of Crystal Bay in Orono Township about 1854.
MINNETONKA — "minne," Sioux for water and "tonka," Sioux for big or great. Governor Ramsey, in 1852, is often given credit for naming the lake.
MINNETONKA BEACH — Surveyed and plotted in 1883 by Adolphus Bode, and given the name of Minnetonka Beach on Lake Minnetonka. Area had been known as Island City.
MINNETRISTA — "minne," Sioux for water and "trista," Sioux for crooked, referring to the two lakes, Dutch and Langdon in the area.
MOUND — first called Mound City, because of the large number of aborigine mounds originally found in the area.
NAVARRE — originally a stop on the Great Northern between Minnetonka Beach and Spring Park. Named by Sam J. Wetherall, early flower lover, because he liked the plumes worn by the Knights of Navarre.
NORENBERG BRIDGE AND ESTATE — 90 acres of north shore on Crystal Bay, owned in the early 1900's by the one-time president of the Grain Belt Brewery. In 1972 the property was willed by his daughter to the Henn County Park Reserve District. The Norenberg bridge crosses passage from Crystal to Maxwell Bay.
NORTHOME — name given to the 200 acres inside the old Northome boulder gate, still standing, that belonged to Sir Charles Gibson of St. Louis. The area was his north home.
ORONO POINT — first called Starvation Point. When George Brackett purchased the point in 1880, he named it Orono for his home town in Maine.
PHELPS ISLAND — sometimes called Island Park . . . Also, Phelps Bay, named for Carrington Phelps, early English settler and developer of the area. O.J. Nobles owned the island earlier.
PRIESTS BAY — named for J.D. Priest, landowner and farmer there in 1876.
ROUND POINT — in Tonka Bay, facing Gideons Bay. The W.O. Winston estate from 1893 — Elizabeth Winston's (Mrs. Fred), summer home.
ROBINSONS BAY — named for A.B. Robinson, an early settler in Wayzata and professional soldier from Vermont.
SAGA HILL — area along northshore drive (#19), west of Forest Lake, and north of West Arm. Theo. Blegen wrote "The Saga of Saga Hill."

TONKA BAY — an abbreviation for Minnetonka. In early days, referred to Gideons Bay. In 1950 the village of Tonka Bay separated from Excelsior, now a city. The land area was called Lake Park in the 1880's.

WAWATASSO ISLAND — Sioux for "Little Firefly" upper lake, touching Indian legend attached to this island. Minneapolis Boy Scouts had their camp here in the 1920s, 30s and 40s. Also called Dunlop Island.

WAYZATA — Sioux for "north shore." The village on the northeast end of the lake first settled in 1852.

WEST POINT — named for E.B. West. Formerly called Wheelers Point. Projects toward the west end of Big Island in Tonka Bay.

WILD GOOSE ISLAND — in upper lake, now a Hennepin County Park, near Spring Park — owned by Ed Reed of Missouri in 1883.

WOODLAND — city, including Maplewood on south shore of Wayzata Bay. The Methodist Assembly grounds are part of it.

WOODSIDE — area between Smithtown Bay and Howards Point on south shore upper lake. Boulder Bridge Farm was located in this section in the 20's and 30's. Recently developed.

ZIMMERMANS PASS (Bridge) — joins Phelps Bay and Cooks Bay. Commodore Zimmerman in 1877 purchased adjoining area.

ZUMBRA HEIGHTS — Overlooking the upper lake near Lake Zumbra. The old Van Dusen home, Algoma Lodge and the old Loring Woodend Farms area.

Much of this glossary was compiled over 30 years ago by area resident and local historian, Russel D. Brackett, and made available by his son, Judd Brackett.

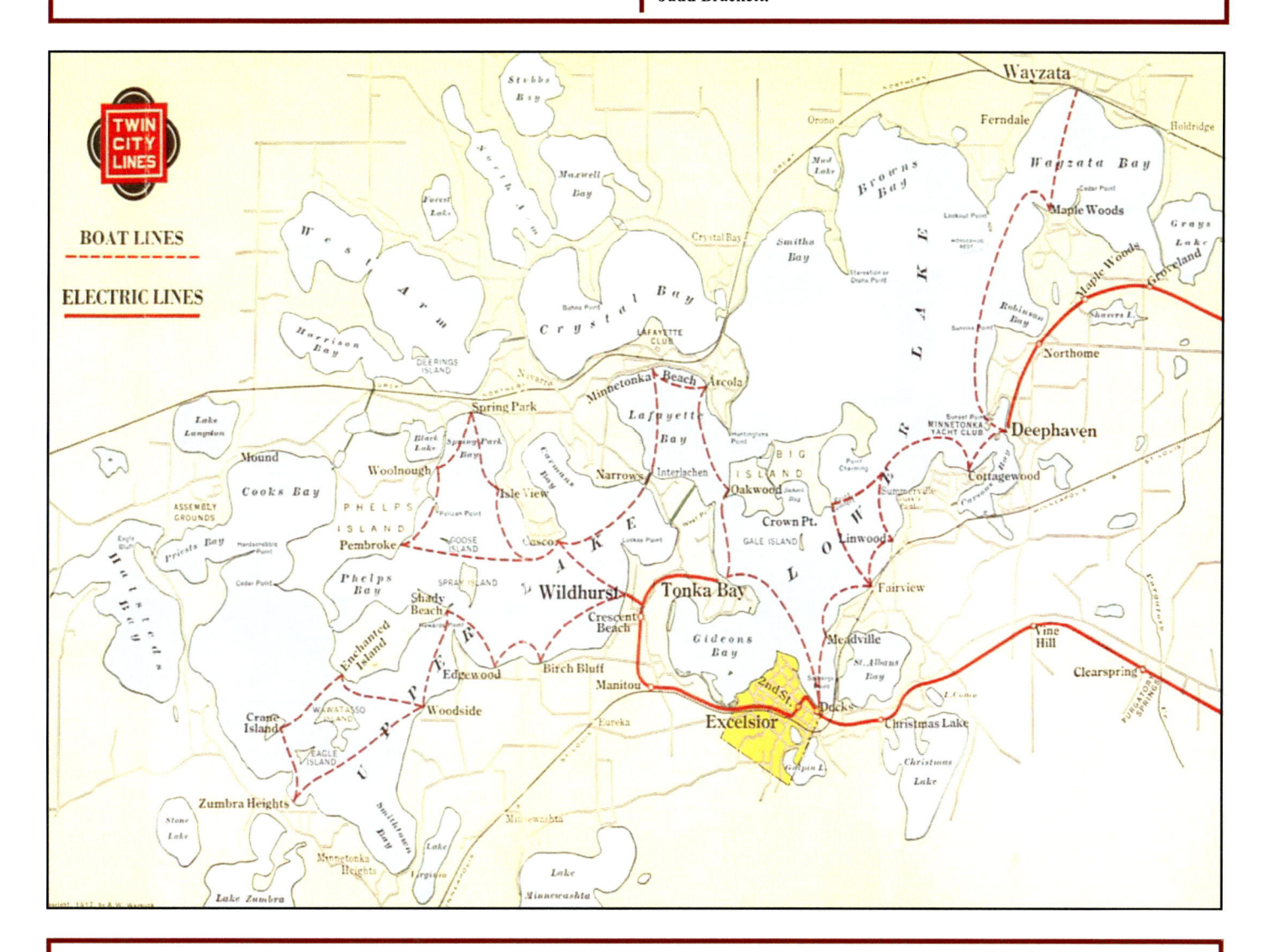

In the language of the Dakota Indians *Minnetonka* means "Big Water." The above map printed on a 1917 Twin Cites Line streetcar brochure gave the following information describing the size of the Big Water. Total area, 21.6 square miles; greatest navigable length for steamboats, Wayzata to Mound, 13.2 miles; greatest width, Deephaven to Crystal Bay, 2.7 miles; total shore line, 125.3 miles, of which 13.9 miles is island frontage. The Upper Lake with a shore line of 42.1 miles, is the largest part, while the Lower Lake has 33.6 miles, and Big Island in its midst has six miles. There are 14 islands in all, of which Phelps Island in the Upper Lake is the largest. There are 24 distinct bays.

A.W. Warnock, General Passenger Agent for the Twin City Lines writes: a quick, pleasant, inexpensive way to skirt Lake Minnetonka's shores and enjoy its varied charms, is to embark on one of the seven speedy Steamboats that make up the unique Fleet owned and operated the Twin City Lines. The route of the Steamboats extends from Zumbra Heights, down through the Upper Lake and the Narrows, into the Lower Lake, and thence from Excelsior along the South shore to Wayzata, a distance of 22 miles. Keeping close to the shore the entire distance, the boats pass many beautiful islands and bays.

In order to look at the interesting and fascinating early history of Lake Minnetonka it is necessary to step back and look not only at the "Glory Years" of the 1880's, but at Minnetonka's very beginning, examine its geological formation and why this is important and how it is so unique.

It is of further interest to look at why the lake became an early favorite of the American Indians, what they called it, and how it remained a secret for so long.

Today, many visitors and residents alike are totally unaware of Lake Minnetonka's illustrious and famous past that included: beloved Indian camp grounds, hundreds of steamboats, one of the oldest yacht clubs in America, two amusement parks, and huge lakefront hotels that attracted world-wide visitors.
Jim Ogland

© DNALGO PUBLICATIONS, WAYZATA, MN 55391

MINNEAPOLIS

ST. PAUL

TWIN CITY LINES

(10)

Huge Hotels at Lake Minnetonka

Minnetonka's Resort Era
The Glory Years

Lake Minnetonka

A HISTORICAL INSIGHT

GRAND HOTELS

By Jim Ogland, author of
"Picturing Lake Minnetonka"

© DNALGO Enterprises Box 935 Wayzata, Mn 55391

HOTELS - A HISTORIC INSIGHT
A chronological record of Minnetonka's early resort and hotel history

THE GLORY YEARS AT LAKE MINNETONKA, 1880's: Stories of beautiful Minnetonka spread widely during the Civil War, and at its conclusion in 1865, visitors from the deep south and elsewhere began arriving. They had heard about the cool summers and the healthful atmosphere. They came by steamboat up the Mississippi, and then by the railroad that would soon reach Wayzata on the northern shore. Encouraged by the large numbers of visitors, hotels, boarding houses and inns sprang up along the shores, each trying to outdo the other. By 1876, over 6000 guests reportedly were registered at five hotels. **The 1880's were clearly the "Glory Years," but by 1893 the tourists from the east and south were going elsewhere.** *"Minnetonka's great resort days were over!"*

A days catch at Lake Minnetonka

Fishing was an important activity for these early visitors. All the hotels had rowboats and equipment for their guests to use. The lake was filled with choice game fish, sunfish, crappies, bass, walleyes, pickerel and perch and the fishing was never disappointing.

First of the early hotels was the *Minnetonka Hotel,* **built in 1853, at Minnetonka Mills.** Essentially, its guests were incoming settlers and mill workers. Because of better accessibility to rail and steamer transportation, many hotels were grouped in or near the lakes three principal towns. **Excelsior** was settled in 1853, **Wayzata** in 1854, with **Mound** incorporating much later in 1912, (however, the *Cook's House* in Mound City was built in 1854.) **Wayzata's first hotel** was the *Harrington Inn* built in **1854** by John Harrington and said to be the first "summer hotel on the lake." It had sixteen rooms and could accommodate up to fourteen year-round guests. Also in Wayzata the same year, was the *Day's Inn* operated by postmaster Abel Day and his wife, Eliza. **The Gleason House,** built in 1865 (originally as the Matteson house), was perhaps the best known Wayzata hotel as it operated for almost a century under the same name.

In Excelsior, the *Galpin Hotel* opened in 1854 and following a disastrous fire, was rebuilt as the *Excelsior house* in 1870. In its first issue (1876) A. S. Diamond's, "Lake Minnetonka Tourist"

The Lake Park Hotel, later named the Tonka Bay Hotel

described the Excelsior House as the largest hotel on the lake with accommodations for over 100 guests. It was enlarged several times and eventually could handle 150 guests. Again in 1876, it was destroyed by fire. On the site, on Memorial Day, 1896, the popular **La Paul House** was opened. At the turn of the century, it was the last word in comfort and convenience.

In Wayzata, in 1870, Captain William Rockwell, piloted the *May Queen,* and in later years

This 1856 watercolor by Englishman, Edwin Whitefield, captures the Excelsior House, near St. Albans Bay, where Whitefield stayed.

the *Belle of Minnetonka.* He along with his brother-in-law, Henry Maurer, built the **Maurer House.** Overlooking the lake at Broadway and Lake Street, this large hotel could easily accommodate 100 guests. The name was changed to the **Minnetonka House,** and later with new ownership, was changed to the **West Hotel.**

In 1860, John Mann built the **Upper Lake House** near Eureka on Edgewood Road. He also acquired the *Sue Gardiner,* the first propeller and the second steamboat on the lake. In 1877, Mann sold the hotel. It was moved to Birch Bluff and eventually became the **Edgewood Hotel.**

In 1880, the Arlington House was Wayzata's largest hotel at a cost of $25,000. It was three stories with over 100 rooms, had a commanding view of the lake, and was located at the eastern end of Wayzata Bay. In 1882, James J. Hill leased the entire hotel and never opened it. It sat empty while Hill opened his gigantic **Lafayette Hotel** at Minnetonka Beach. The Arlington House never reopened and burned to the ground six years later.

The **Maple Heights Inn** was located on Island Park facing Spring Park Bay and overlooked Goose Island. It was owned and managed in the **1880's** by J.H.Woolnough, later called Woolnoughs, and even later, Tippiwauken. It operated into the 1960's.

The White House

The **White House** in Excelsior (1872-1946) was situated in a very prominent location facing the bay at the corner of Lake and Water Streets. Guests relaxed on the large porch and enjoyed the wonderful lake breezes. It was a landmark and served the community for many years.

Every room in the Hotel Lafayette was equipped with a fire-extinguishing grenade like the one shown here. Its chemical contents were intended to snuff out a fire when thrown at the base of a fire. On the morning of October 4, 1897, fire broke out in the hotel which was closed for the season. Fanned by high winds it was quickly destroyed. Local papers reported that "men threw numerous grenades to no avail."

Fire Grenade

The **Hotel Harrow** was built by Major Thomas Harrow in 1879, and opened in **1880.** Located on **Shady Island** this comfortable hotel could handle 150 guests and featured great fishing. It was best accessible by steamer. The nearby **Palmer House** was a popular location catering to those desiring a healthful resort.

(14)

Lake Park Hotel at Tonka Bay   1879 - 1913

The huge **Lake Park Hotel was built in 1879** and opened originally as a part of the then popular *Chautaugua* movement. After the first year, however, it began catering to patrons visiting the lake for health and other reasons. Originally named the **Minnetonka Park Hotel**, it was changed to the **Lake Park Hotel**, then to its most recognized name, the **Tonka Bay Hotel**. At the time, it was the largest hotel at *Lake Minnetonka* and with its many amenities, was always a great favorite. A third story was added increasing the capacity to 1000 guests, with the dining room seating 400 patrons at one time. In 1907, it was acquired by the *Twin City Rapid Transit Company* as a part of their expanding plans for Lake Minnetonka. With a boat shuttle between the hotel and their new picnic grounds at Big Island, they were able to cater hot meals and serve large groups very effectively. *At least six trains arrived and departed daily on a branch line of the M & St. L. Railroad with the depot just a two-minute walk.*

Pictured on the right, is the wharf that numerous steamboats docked at each day. The large white building is the pavilion/casino, a theater for plays, ballroom dancing and other entertainment. It later became the roller rink. The hotel can be seen in the background.

In the spring of 1908, the streetcar line was extended from Excelsior, making it possible to ride directly from Minneapolis to the *Tonka Bay Hotel*. The grounds were extensive, and included horse stables, walkways, tennis courts and bicycle trails.

In 1911, the hotel closed for good, along with all operations at the Big Island Amusement Park, **including dismantling of the three ferry boats and all the excursion boats.** The casino building was disassembled in 1920, and given by Horace Lowry, President of the TCRT, to Excelsior. It was moved by barge, (some reports say that it was moved on the ice) to Excelsior and became a popular dance hall (Big Reggie's Danceland).

St. Louis Hotel at Deephaven   1879-1907

Opening in 1879, Hotel St. Louis was the first large hotel on Lake Minnetonka. Sir Charles Gibson, a successful St. Louis lawyer, first discovered the beauty and charm of Lake Minnetonka in 1870, when he acquired land for his northern vacation home. Following the completion of "*Northhome*," the name given to his northern vacation home, Sir Charles decided to build a hotel to accommodate his many friends from St. Louis and other southern cities. The site picked for the hotel overlooked Bay St. Louis and Carsons Bay, and was served by two railroads. A branch of the Chicago, Milwaukee and St. Paul Railway came right to the door of the hotel. The Minneapolis and St. Louis Railway (M&St.L.) brought passengers to the depot at nearby Deephaven, where waiting carriages transported guests and visitors to the hotel. Like other hotels that followed, the St. Louis was wood frame construction. It was three stories in height, with open porches on each level. Its 200 rooms were comfortably furnished and eventually boasted modern electric lights. It was an impressive structure situated on high ground with grand views of the lake and the Yacht Club on Light House Island. It was painted a light gray with green trim **and had a bath on every floor.**

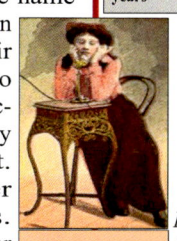

Carsons Bay from Hotel St. Louis

The St. Louis Hotel across the bay

In **1901 telephones could be found at these locations:**
Hotel Del Otero
Lake Park Hotel
Hotel St. Louis
Mtka Beach
Cottagewood Hotel
Wayzata
Excelsior

Hotel del Otero at Spring Park   1885-1945

A handbook of Lake Minnetonka published in 1901 had the following to say about the Hotel del Otero: "*The point to which most transient visitors direct their steps is Spring Park station and the Hotel del Otero. This is a beautifully built and well managed summer hotel, with numbers of large and airy rooms overlooking the lake. It has large wide piazzas, screened to keep out insects, is supplied with fresh water from the lake, piped to all the rooms, has all modern conveniences in the way of bathrooms, electric lights, etc. The boat house run in connection with the hotel, keeps at all times a fleet of forty or fifty well appointed rowboats, sailboats of various kinds and gasoline launches are always available. Steamers meet all arriving trains at Wayzata and visitors may leave the boat at Spring Park, have their lunch in the cool pleasant dining room of the Hotel and return to the city by afternoon train.*"

The Del Otero Hotel operated at the lake for over 60 years

The casino with hotel in background

"**There isn't a more delightful place to spend a summer outing than at Lake Minnetonka.** The hotel annually hosts the legendary "grocers' picnic" on its large picnic grounds. Sweeping views of Spring Park Bay from the hotel windows are spectacular and it is a perfect setting. The hotel is usually full, so reserve early."

(15)

Copyright DNALGO Enterprises Box 935 Wayzata, Mn 55391

The Hotel Lafayette

The Hotel Lafayette was the largest hotel ever built at Lake Minnetonka

Hotel location at Minnetonka Beach

The Hotel Lafayette opened on Sunday, July 2, 1882, with great pomp and celebration.

James J. Hill about 1910

James J. Hill was known as the "Empire Builder," but he was also a builder of fine hotels. At Lake Minnetonka he built two great hotels: the huge *Hotel Lafayette* at Minnetonka Beach and the *Hotel Del Otero* at Spring Park. At the time the Lafayette was advertised as "The finest hotel west of New York City."

All 300 rooms were occupied, as it was the highlight of the social season, and an event that would be long remembered. Music throughout the hotel and the grounds, was provided by strolling musicians and orchestras that played late into the night. By 1882, Lake Minnetonka was well on its way to becoming one of the nation's most popular vacation spots for the south's super-rich. Wishing to escape the intense summer heat, vacationers from the deep south, and as far away as Europe, flocked to Lake Minnetonka.

Though not the first to build a hotel at the lake, Hill's was the biggest and most luxurious ever built at Lake Minnetonka.

The Lafayette was mammoth and became a spectacular addition to the already huge hotels at Lake Minnetonka. The building alone was 745 feet in length, almost 100 feet wide, and rising 90 feet in height. It towered over the lakeshore that faced in two directions. It was an enormous structure that used over 3 million board feet of lumber, carloads of nails, hundreds of squares of red cedar wood shingles, and the interior was plastered throughout. It was stained a dark olive green color that added to its already immense look. The area surrounding the hotel when it opened, was rather naked and devoid of any trees. Hill earlier logged off the once dense standing timber to provide fuel for a shortage that had developed in

The largest boat on the lake in 1882 was the *"City of St. Louis" and* was associated with the St. Louis Hotel. Steamboats were an important means of lake transportation. Not to be outdone, Hill built the incredible 300 ft, 2500 passenger *"Belle of Minnetonka,"* shown here.

the Twin Cities during the severe winter of 1872.

The hotel quickly became the social center for much of the lake, and over the years entertained many celebrities, including two presidents. Chester A. Arthur visited in 1883, and Ulysses S. Grant reportedly visited the Lafayette twice.

The following advertisement appeared on the back of a advertising photo postcard. "The house is capable of accommodating over 900 guests and is supplied with all the conveniences of a modern hotel. It has an elevator, gas in every room, and electric lights throughout the house and grounds. ***The hotel is situated on a peninsula, and is so surrounded with water that every room faces the lake.*** *The hotel has the finest lawn tennis courts in the northwest. Grand tournaments, and elegant prizes will be given. A bowling alley, billiards, dancing halls and baseball grounds are provided. The fishing on Lake Minnetonka can not be surpassed. Bass, pickerel, crappies, sunfish, etc. are available in undiminished numbers. An elegant line of steamers, with accommodations for over 5,000 people, has been established on Lake Minnetonka. A plentiful supply of sail will be one of the features of the house. The reputation of the hotel for the excellent music furnished*

Fire destroys the famous Hotel Lafayette: The Minneapolis Tribune of October 5, 1897, says: "The hotel was totally destroyed by fire yesterday."

(16)

HOTEL DEL OTERO

SPRING PARK

JAMES J. HILL'S SECOND HOTEL at Lake Minnetonka was built three years after the Hotel Lafayette (1885), and was intended to draw patrons farther west on the Great Northern Railway. This was standard operation for railroads of the period as they built *destination resort locations* to attract railroad ridership. **The Del Otero was a great destination.** It not only was a large, well equipped hotel, but it had a fine casino at lakeside, and huge picnic grounds for events of any size.

The Del Otero out-lived all the other major hotels, and was still serving guests almost 50 years after the Lafayette burned to the ground.

The casino was a wonderful place that had many amenities. It was first of all a dancing pavilion, with regular dance bands that played to capacity crowds on summer weekends well into the 1940's. Young neighborhood boys earned good money setting pins at its three popular bowling lanes. It had a cocktail bar and a restaurant on the main level, while the downstairs was open to serve

The Del Otero Hotel was a landmark at the lake for over 60 years

the best swimming beach in the area. On hot summer days, patrons of all ages frolicked in the water and slid down the water slide or swam out to the swimming raft. Everyone wore heavy wool swimsuits, and the ladies wore swimming caps.

Fishing equipment and dark green freshly painted rowboats were available to rent. Worms, minnows and frogs were also available, as were experienced fishing guides. The picnic grounds were huge, covering many acres, with enough space for even the largest of picnics. The annual *"grocers' picnics"* were legendary. With the grounds overlooking Spring Park Bay, and the islands in the distance, it was an idyllic setting. The hotel itself had two large dining rooms and an enormous kitchen capable of serving hotel guests and large banquets with the finest cuisine. In addition several guest cottages were available for rent, some of which are still there today in private ownership. On July 16, 1945, after a social evening by a crowd of military brass, the hotel somehow, about 3:30 a.m., caught fire and swept by high winds, burnt to the ground.

FIRST OF THE GRAND HOTELS
TONKA BAY HOTEL and the ST. LOUIS HOTEL, Est 1879

The Lake Park Hotel, established in 1879, later became the Tonka Bay Hotel. It had a commanding view of the lower lake with a slogan, **"Every room on a veranda."** It quickly became a very popular resort and with accommodations for over 1000 guests, there was always a lot of activity. Today it is hard to imagine the anticipation and excitement created by the arriving trains and steamboats! The amusement pavilion had a ballroom and a theater for summer operas and plays.

Tonka Bay Hotel in the background with the Casino on the right

The ST. LOUIS HOTEL
The first large hotel at Lake Minnetonka

The St. Louis ushered in the "Glory Years" of the 1880's and led the way for wealthy tourists from the south to visit Lake Minnetonka. Most of its guests came from New Orleans, St. Louis, Kansas City and other southern cities. It was an imposing structure, built on a hill over looking Carson's Bay and the Minnetonka Yacht Club, in Bay St. Louis. It had verandas on each of its three levels with sweeping views of the lake. It was serviced by two railroads and numerous steamboats from nearby Excelsior and Wayzata.

(18)

Eventually there were over 60 hotels, *now there are none!*

One of the principal hotels on the lower lake was the **"Keewaydin Hotel"** built in **1885**. It was located at Deephaven in Cottagewood. Initially known as the *Cottagewood Club House*, re-named *Keeywaydin* after the city paid half the cost of a new public dock. It was a lovely place with a large dining room and good food. Some years later it was enlarged to have forty sleeping rooms.

Keeywaydin Hotel

With its sturdy dock, the Keewaydin became a regular stop for the new "Express Boats." Like so many other hotels it was unfortunately destroyed by fire in 1924.

Excelsior was not only home port to numerous steamboats, but to a number of hotels located right in town. Among them were the **Sampson House, (1895)** and the **La Paul Hotel, (1896).**

The **Sampson House** was built and rebuilt several times following fires and changes in ownership. Its most lasting image, **1895**, is the one shown here. Finally closing in 1960, the venerable hotel is said to be the last survivor of some 20 Excelsior Hotels.

The **La Paul Hotel** was a large three-story structure, that in addition to the hotel, housed Dr. La Paul's medical practice. It had many modern conveniences, including hot water heat. La Paul also owned and operated the steamboat, *"George,"* which when launched not only was unsightly, but almost capsized. It was rebuilt as the *"Excelsior"* and became a very successful excursion boat. The *"Excelsior"* was publicly burned in the summer of 1910, and despite a steady drizzle, drew a large crowd.

The Maple Heights Inn / Tippiwauken

Mound had a surprising number of moderately priced family hotels.
Among them were the **Cook's House**, later known as the **Lake View House**. It was here that some of the earliest town meetings were held. **The Dewey House** was located eastward along the shore and was a quiet and healthful place with low rates. The **Mound City Hotel** was a smaller comfortable hotel that opened in **1884**. Another well known hotel was the **Palmer House** located at Zumbra Heights. It was billed as a health resort.

The Chapman House opened with a bang on the Fourth of July, 1876. A typical family summer resort with good food and great fishing, it soon became one of the most popular hotels on the Upper Lake. It was large with rooms on three floors and could accommodate fifty guests. It had a wonderful bathing beach and docking for numerous boats. In 1906, a large pavilion was built on the property just steps away from the waterfront. It became known as the

Mound Casino and in later years as the *Surfside*. The second level was a huge roller skating rink which was used for dances and wedding receptions. It remained a popular restaurant and night spot into the 1980's.

Bartlett Place Hotel, 1883: A 1901 advertisement for the Upper Lake, Mound Hotel said the following: "This is becoming a very popular place for bicyclists to lunch, and many wheel here for a day's fishing. The waters at this end of the lake abound with fish. Bait and oarsman are always at hand."

Moonlight excursions, sailing, rowing and dancing, are part of the excitement. The cuisine service of this hotel is strictly first class.

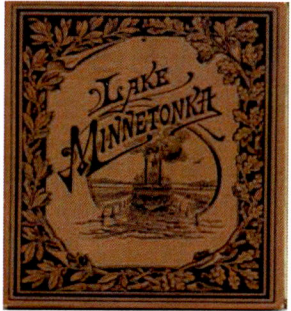

Souvenir booklets and folders were purchased and saved as cherished mementos of a special trip or Minntonka vacation

Vacationers and day trippers primarily arrived by one of the railroads that served the area, or by one of the numerous steamboats that provided transportation around the lake. Many of the hotels had their own steam launches that met the arriving trains. Later on in 1906, the streetcar company implemented numerous routes for their unique fast Express Boats. If signaled, they stopped at any dock.

The Buena Vista Hotel

Located westward from Chapman's in the Mound Highlands, it was a relative latecomer to Lake Minnetonka **(1903-1926.)** It was never-the-less, a very popular summer hotel catering to vacationers who wanted a quiet, restful time. Like many of the lake hotels, its appearance changed periodically over the years as additions were added.

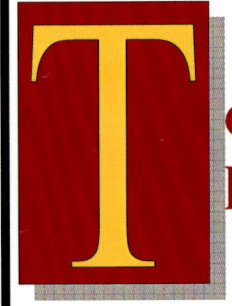

The lake was soon dotted with hotels. Many of them were just summer places and often had cottages as well. Most were built in the 1850's thru the 1890's.

Some of the more noted ones were located on:

Lower Lake

Minnetonka Hotel, Mtka. Mills 1853
Days Inn, Wayzata 1854
Harrington House, Wayzata 1854
Newark Hotel, Mtka. Mills 1857
Well-Come Inn, Excelsior 1858
Maplewood Inn, Deephaven 1869
Gleason House, Wayzata 1865
Minnetonka House, Wayzata 1870
White House, Excelsior 1872
Mix Hill House, St. Albans Bay 1877
St. Louis Hotel, Deephaven 1879
Lake Park Hotel, Tonka Bay 1879
Arlington House, Wayzata 1880
Lafayette Hotel, Mtka. Beach 1882
Donaldson House, Excelsior 1880's
Keeywaydin, Cottagewood 1885
Sampson House, Excelsior 1895
La Paul Hotel, Excelsior 1896
Maple Inn, Excelsior 1901
Northland Inn, Wayzata 1901
St. Albans Hotel, St. Albans Bay 1912

Upper Lake

Edgewood Hotel, Eureka 1860
Chapman House, Mound 1876
Lakeview House, Mound 1876
Harrow Hotel, Shady Island 1880
Palmer House, Zumbra 1880
Maple Heights Inn, Island Park 1880's
Bartlett House, Mound 1883
Mound City Hotel, Mound 1884
Del Otero Hotel, Spring Park 1885
Dewey Cottage, Mound 1899
Buena Vista Hotel, Mound 1902

CHAPMAN HOUSE
The Chapman House is probably the best known and most popular hotel on Lake Minnetonka, and is one of the oldest. Situated at the very head of the lake, the location is retired and at the same time accessible. The house stands upon a bluff about 25 feet above the water, commanding a splendid view of the upper lake, and is surrounded by a forest of large trees and a luxuriant growth of grass, forming a natural park seven acres in extent.
CHAPMANS FOR FISH
The fishing at Chapmans is famous all over the country. As the upper lake is less frequented than the lower, the fish are naturally more plentiful. Boats, fishing tackle and bait always at hand.

Rates: $7.00 to $10.00 per Week

Information was gathered from several sources, including S.E. Ellis,' "Picturesque Minnetonka" Tourist Guides, and the 1899 National Health Journal (Special Minnetonka Edition). Dates are when the first structure was built, possibly under a different name.

Advertisement (1899)

Because of better accessiblity to rail or steamer transportation, many hotels were grouped in the three major towns: Wayzata, Excelsior and Mound. Many started as boarding houses with just a few rooms, but as lodging demands and business prospered, they added on. Some added not only a few rooms, but entire second and even third floors. **Often the names of establishments were known as either houses or hotels interchangeably.**

Steamboatin'

Incredible steamboats of the 1880's

Lake Minnetonka

A HISTORICAL INSIGHT

STEAMBOATS

By Jim Ogland, author of
"Picturing Lake Minnetonka"

DNALGO Enterprises Box 935 Wayzata, Mn 55391

(23)

STEAMBOATIN'

This was the incredible steamboat era of the 1880's. They provided transportation not only on the rivers and waterways throughout America, but also in ever increasing numbers at Lake Minnetonka. Shortly after the end of the Civil War, as more and more tourists began arriving, the need for better transportation to and from the hotels, inns and boarding houses became apparent. *Many of the smaller hotels had their own steamers, however, most did not.* They relied instead on the lake steamers to bring arriving guests from the train stations to their hotels. In addition to carrying "arriving and departing" passengers, the steamers delivered building materials and other supplies to locations all around the lake. Some of the boats were used primarily for charters or lake excursions. Others such as the *City of St. Louis and the Belle of Minnetonka* were essentially built to carry passengers to and from their respective hotels, *the St. Louis and the Hotel Lafayette*.

Photo courtesy of the Minnesota Historical Society
Excursion steamboats were always popular and generally crowded with eager sightseers, many visiting Minnetonka for the first time were anxious to explore the lake.

The *Excelsior, Victor and Puritan*, pictured here arriving at the Tonka Bay Hotel, also brought guests and tourists to many of the other hotels around the lake.

HOME TO OVER NINETY STEAMBOATS: Before it was over, almost one hundred steamboats would call Minnetonka home. From the smallest to the largest, each boat had its own personality, its own temperament, and its own legends. **The first steamboat arrived at the Wayzata docks on the northern shore of Lake Minnetonka in the year 1860.** It was built by a ship's carpenter for the Reverend Charles Galpin of Excelsior and was named the *"Governor Ramsey."* The flat bottom, fifty foot sidewheeler was the beginning of the incredible era of steamboats, railroads and large hotels. After a few years, the race was on to see who could build the biggest, the fastest, the most luxurious steamboat. The large hotels competed with each other for business and their steamboats were an important part of their overall image. More importantly, they provided transportation to and from the railroad stations for the increasing number of visitors and vacationers. The steamboats reached their zenith in 1881 when the *"City of St. Louis"* was constructed at Wayzata. It was one hundred and sixty feet long, forty feet wide and carried over one thousand passengers. Not to be outdone, James J. Hill builder of the enormous Lafayette Hotel, launched the *"Belle of Minnetonka,"* With a length of 300 feet and a beam of sixty, *it was the largest boat ever built at Lake Minnetonka.* It had a capacity for twenty five hundred passengers. **An intense rivalry quickly developed between the two boats.** After meeting the trains in Wayzata they would square off and race across the seven miles of open water to Excelsior. With smoke billowing from their stacks and with their engines pounding, they were off to Minnetonka Beach and the upper lake.

BEAUTIFUL LAKE MINNETONKA

Steamboat Tonka - 1878-1900 Originally named the *Hattie May*, first stern wheeler on the lake. Shown at Spring Park

The Glory Years had arrived! Lake Minnetonka would never again be the same. *It was the dawn of an exciting, wonderful, and marvelous era.* Countless thousands of tourists and visitors would ride the magnificent steamboats before it was over. To see the boats lined up at the Wayzata docks awaiting the trains, blowing their whistles in anticipation, was a sight to behold. Families from the South arrived with what seemed like endless quantities of luggage and servants. They came for the summer and they came for a good time!

The huge side-wheeler, *Belle of Minnetonka*, was constructed at Wayzata in 1882 following shipment from the Mississippi River where it had operated for a number of years. It was originally named the *"Phil Sheridan."* It arrived in sections that included its machinery, engines, stacks, etc. Launched for trials on July 3, 1882, it was immediately challenged by the *"City of St. Louis."* The *Belle* operated until 1892 and was finally dismantled in 1898 at St. Albans Bay. Its bell was rescued and installed in the belfry of the Excelsior Schoolhouse.

The 300ft. triple deck, 2500 passenger "Belle of Minnetonka"

With the 1882 launching of the huge "Belle of Minnetonka" came the beginning of an incredible 10 year rivalry with the "City of St. Louis."

(24)

THE "CITY OF ST LOUIS"

Photo of the City of St. Louis courtesy of the Minnesota Historical Society, Circa: 1895

was launched at Wayzata, June 4, 1881. It was owned by Minneapolis and St. Louis Railroad President, W.D. Washburn, who was also affiliated with the Hotel St. Louis. The hull was built in Jefferson, Indiana, and shipped to Wayzata where its upper decks and cabin were added by local shipwrights and carpenters. Native lumber was used throughout. The cabin interior was finished in beautiful mahogany, at **160 feet in length, it was at the time, the largest boat ever built at Lake Minnetonka.** It was the first inland lake vessel in the United States to be equipped with electricity. Built to river specifications, it drew only sixteen inches, even when loaded with its full capacity of one thousand passengers. The "City" was completely overhauled in 1895, and just three years later, during the winter of 1898/99, it was totally dismantled. Lake Minnetonka's most famous Captain was **Capt'n John R. Johnson,** captain of the *City of St. Louis.* Born in Norway in 1859, and while visiting a relative in Minnesota in 1880, he by chance met W. D. Washburn, who explained that he was planning to build the *City of St Louis* the following year. He offered Johnson a job to help build and operate the new boat. Johnson cancelled plans to return to Norway and the sea, and instead, accepted the offer.

He eventually became the captain of the City of St. Louis and a Lake Minnetonka legend as well. Captain Johnson was associated with the lake and steamboats the rest of his life. In 1898, he began to assemble his own fleet using the name L.M.T. Co. He owned the steamer, *Alert,* acquired the 100ft sternwheeler, *Hattie May,* changing its name to the *Tonka,* and purchased the steamer, *Saucy Kate,* and the tug, *Dagmar.* He built the 70ft *Mayflower* and the 85ft *Puritan.* He also owned the 48ft tug, *Priscilla,* and built the 75ft *Plymouth* in 1903. Very much involved in lake dredging, he owned a number of tugs and companion barges. In 1906, he sold the excursion steamers *Puritan, Mayflower,* and the *Plymouth* to the Minneapolis & St. Paul Street Railway Company, which was acquiring their own fleet to be used in conjunction with the developing Big Island Picnic and Amusement Park operation. This group, using the name "Minnetonka & White Bear Navigation Co.," also operated the famous new Express Boats, (Streetcar Boats) and the Big Island ferrys. The formation of the M&WB NAV Co. signaled the end of other steamboats on the lake and within a few years all others were gone. Captain Johnson died in Excelsior on March 19, 1931.

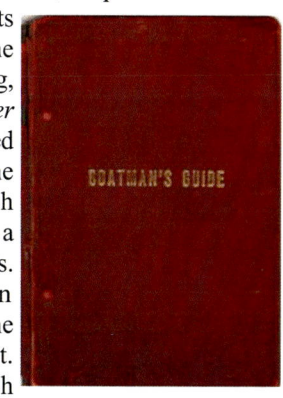

Lake Minnetonka Steamers

In 1860, the Reverend Charles Galpin of Excelsior, saw the need for a faster way to get from place to place around the densely wooded lake. He hired a carpenter to build a boat and named it the *Governor Ramsey*. It wasn't the most attractive boat, but the fifty foot side-wheeler was soon carrying not only passengers, but mail, food, and building supplies to all points on the lake.

For eight years the *Governor Ramsey* ruled, un-challenged, as the only passenger steamboat on the lake. In 1867, it met the first train at Wayzata.

A rival appeared in 1868: The smaller 35ft *Sue Gardiner* had been built in Detroit and unlike the Governor, it had a propeller. This was the first time that a non paddlewheel steamboat was used on the lake. It was purchased by hotel owner, John Mann, and became an important addition to his hotel, the Edgewood.

The Sue Gardiner—lakes first propeller

A twenty-eight foot propeller, christened the *Minnetrista*, was launched at the lake in 1869. It was followed by the *Fresco*, owned by Charles Burwell, and for a number of years operated from Minnetonka Mills.

Prelude to the "Glory Years" The 1870's at Lake Minnetonka

In 1873, the 65 ft steamboat, *May Queen,* said to be the best looking and fastest boat on the lake, was constructed for Captain Wm Rockwell. The sale and departure of the *Sue Gardiner* to Lake Pepin in 1875, left the *May Queen* as the only passenger steamboat on the lake. The *May Queen* needed competition and it came in 1876, with the completion of the 78 ft propeller, *Mary*. Built by Civil War naval veteran, Capt Frank Halstead, it quickly challenged the May Queen. Starting in Wayzata, they raced daily on the same routes vying for cargo and passengers. Both boats had the same type boiler and both eventually met similar fates. The *May Queen's* boiler suddenly exploded while docked at Shady Island and injured several people. The *Mary* exploded on July 1, 1880, at the St. Louis Hotel dock killing two people and injuring eight. Eventually it was determined that the boiler design was faulty. **In 1876, the** *Seventy Six* became the first boat actually built as a tug. Unfortunately it had the same Ames boiler as the *Mary* and the *May Queen,* and it too exploded. It was rebuilt as the Hercules and later burned at Casco Point. Like so many others, it was rebuilt numerous times, had many names and several owners, before dismantling in 1898.

The May Queen

By the end of the decade, a small number of steamers had appeared on the lake. They were mostly associated with Captain May, who was acquiring quite a fleet. The 54 ft, side-wheeler, *Rambler,* was built in 1874 and was said to be able to run on a heavy dew. It was used primarily to carry grain and other products from Excelsior to Minnetonka Mills. The 45ft *Kate* was built as a tug in 1876 and used essentially in the Upper Lake. After only one season, it was rebuilt to carry passengers and renamed the *Katie May*. **It was outfitted with a new boiler, and following a brief period of operation, the boiler exploded killing the Captain, Engineer and a passenger.** The wreck was salvaged, restructured and renamed the *Saucy Kate*. Eventually it was purchased by the new Lake Minnetonka Navigation Company (L.M.N.C.) and remained operational, until burning off Solberg's Point in 1899. The first steamboat, acquired by the Lake Minnetonka Navigational Company in 1880, was the 45ft propeller, *Nautilus*. It had previously been launched in 1878 as the *Lulu*.

The popular excursion boat, *Plymouth,* a 75ft double decker with a capacity for 100 passengers, was built in Excelsior.

Minnesota Historical Society Photo

At the turn of the decade, Lake Minnetonka was fast becoming a popular vacation destination for wealthy Southerners and guests from the Eastern United States. Hotels and inns were quickly springing up around the lake. The huge Lake Park Hotel at Tonka Bay had just opened as did the Hotel St. Louis at Deephaven. They were followed in 1882 by the enormous Hotel Lafayette at Minnetonka Beach. **The 1880's saw a new surge in steam transportation. Railroads brought visitors to the lake and the steamboats provided quick, efficient transportation to the hotels and boarding houses.**

Compound-condensing steam engines and improved boilers were gradually being introduced into the lakes steamboats. Prior to this, the engines were the more dangerous high-pressure engines. The *Rosander* was the first steamboat on Minnetonka to have a compound-condensing engine. *Compounding* means that multiple cylinders reuse the same steam to increase the power of the engine, thus compounding it. *Condensing* means that the used steam is allowed to cool in a condenser and condense back into water to be reheated and converted again to steam in the boiler.

Viewed from the Excelsior city docks, this scene was repeated daily. The boats have just left the city docks and the *City of St Louis* (on the left), is racing with the larger *Belle of Minnetonka*, to the Hotel Lafayette. The smaller steamboat in the center is the *Lotus*, that often tagged along and raced with the big boats. They had earlier met the arriving trains in Wayzata and raced across the seven miles of open water to Excelsior. Typically the *City*, being smaller and more maneuverable, got turned around and underway quicker then the *Belle*. The *Belle*, however, was bigger and faster and usually caught up to the *City* and won the race. After leaving the Hotel Lafayette they would go through the Narrows and the Upper Lake on to Chapmans at Mound.

Photo Courtesy of the Minnesota Historical Society
Small steamers waiting for passengers at the Lafayette Hotel dock are ready to depart for various points around the lake. Notice the coal bin in the foreground.

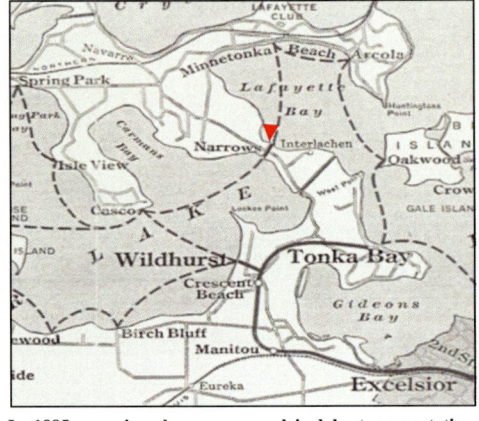

In 1885, a major change occurred in lake transportation. The dredging of the long awaited new Narrows was finally completed. This new channel connecting the Upper and Lower Lake allowed even the largest passenger steamboats, the *Belle of Minnetonka* and the *City of St, Louis* access to Spring Park, Mound, Zumbra and the entire upper lake. The narrow, weedy old Narrows was abandoned. It can still be seen today a few blocks east of the present narrows. With the opening of the connection to the Upper Lake a great number of small steamers and launches appeared on the lake.

(26)

the Glory Years... 1880's, 90's

From the beginning of the 1880's through the early 1890's, many of America's wealthiest families visited Lake Minnetonka. Some came to escape the suffocating heat of the summer South, others from as far away as Europe. They came by train and by Mississippi River steamboats. Most arrived in Wayzata with loads of baggage, many with nannies and servants. These were the *Glory Days* at Lake Minnetonka.

Bustling Wayzata docks in 1881: Pictured are the *Hattie May, Minneapolis, Lotus* and *City of St. Louis*.

These prosperous times created the need for many new hotels and lodging places, which in turn brought a great demand for additional steamboats. They soon arrived, large and small.

The *Belle of Minnetonka*: Assembled at Minnetonka in 1882

Pictured below is the *Excelsior*, one of only a few stern-wheelers on the lake. It was originally built as the *George* by George La Paul, who operated the La Paul Hotel in Excelsior. It was *unsightly and almost capsized when launched*. Re-built as the *Excelsior*, it became a popular excursion boat until it was eventually burned as a public event one summer evening in 1910. Despite poor weather it drew a large crowd.

Excelsior at Hotel Del Otero dock: Spring Park

The majority of Minnetonka Steamboats appeared on the lake during the 1880's - close to one hundred boats before it was over. (See list & dates on last page.)

It has been said that, "without steamboats Minnetonka could never have had its "Glory Years." With steamboats, it rose from an obscure fishing lake to one of the most recognizable vacation spots in all of America. Steam transportation, however, was not without hazards. Numerous boiler explosions causing injury and even death occurred at the lake with some frequency. Perhaps the greatest disaster of all was the sinking of the thirty five foot *Minnie Cook*.

Following are a few early 1880's steamboats:
Flying Dutchman, Florence Deering, Nina, Forest Queen, Grace, Nellie May, Jeanette, Lotus, Rosander, Dot, Hawkeye, Nellie May, Minnesota, Maplewood, Signal, Wayzata, Florence Wright,

Tragedy on the Lake
It was Sunday afternoon, July 12, 1885, the weather was pleasant and the lake was busy with activity. Former Minneapolis Mayor Alonzo Rand, along with seven members of his family, and a family friend had chartered the steamer, *Minnie Cook*, to take them on an afternoon tour to the upper lake. They spent about an hour on Shady Island laughing and having a good time. About 3:30 the sky began to darken and everyone scurried back aboard the boat. The engineer, George McDonald, quickly set course for Wayzata Bay. Unknown to them, a gale was brewing and they were racing a powerful storm. By the time they were approaching Spirit Knob, the waves were several feet high and the

Wayzata Bay

little craft broached, then capsized. The *Minnie Cook* sank off Maplewood with all aboard. As the storm blew by, more than 100 boats raced to the area to no avail. All ten passengers had drowned including Mayor and Mrs. Rand. Grappling-hooks brought the bodies to the surface and the recovered boat was put back into service almost immediately. Just two weeks later, the *Minnie Cook* almost floundered again. This time it was taken to Excelsior where it was dismantled and converted to a barge.

TURN OF THE CENTURY

By 1890, the halcyon days of the 1880's at Lake Minnetonka were coming to a close. In 1892, the *Belle* remained tied to the dock for the entire season. **Minnetonka's great resort days were over!** The lake was more or less forgotten as a tourist attraction. Then suddenly in 1905, streetcars from the Twin Cities rolled into Excelsior. Along with them, came an incredibly exciting and ambitious plan by Thomas Lowry and his Twin City Rapid Transit Company to build an amusement park on Big Island.

Streetcars on the Lake

A new era of transportation had arrived. Six unique torpedo stern "Express" boats were built in the streetcar company shops at 31st and Nicollet and launched in April and May of 1906. Like their streetcar cousins, they were painted bright yellow and quickly became the darlings of the lake. They were named after Twin City area streetcar lines, *Como, Harriet, Hopkins, Stillwater, White Bear* and *Minnehaha*. Operating for over twenty years, they provided transportation to all points of the lake. A seventh boat, the *Excelsior*, was added in 1915. By then the jaunty yellow boats were called streetcar boats or sometimes yellow jackets. They initially operated daily on four scheduled routes and sometimes helped to bring patrons to the evening music concerts held on Big Island. In addition to the streetcar boats, the TCRT acquired several large excursion boats which provided daily tours in both the upper and lower lake. They were

Steam gauges on the restored six ton Minnehaha engine.

also available for charter. Foreseeing a need to transport large numbers of visitors to the Big Island Picnic and Amusement Park, they also built three 142ft ferry boats. Each ferry could accommodate one thousand passengers. They were double-ended, meaning they could go in either direction without turning around. On weekends and holidays, one left the Excelsior docks for the island every twenty minutes. **It was not to last.** The amusement park closed in 1911, and the excursion and ferry boats were dismantled, burned or sunk. The streetcar boats held on until 1926, when they too were dismantled or sunk in deep water off Big Island. The *Hopkins* survived as a excursion boat until 1949 when it too was sunk. **And then they were all gone!**

UP FROM THE DEPTHS: After years of searching, diver Jerry Provost finally located a sunken Streetcar Boat. The water was 60 ft deep, visibility was poor (only about 2ft), and the water cool in the mid-summer of 1979. There was no mistaking it! This was the long sought after discovery of one of the elusive, Express Boats of the once famous fleet of Streetcar Steamboats sunk in 1926. **In the summer of 1980, the thought of raising the discovered steamboat began to be discussed.** It would be a challenging and difficult operation. A large barge was positioned and anchored over the site. The divers secured straps under the hull and with the use of large air bags and cranes the boat was finally brought to the surface.

A Second Chance: After the boat was pulled from the lake and allowed to dry out, the name gradually appeared on the bow. *It was the Minnehaha!* In 1990 the Minnesota Transportation Museum took title to the boat and began planning a total restoration. Local volunteers worked more than 80,000 man-hours and raised thousands of dollars to complete the six year restoration. On May 25, 1996, one of the lakes legendary steamboats completed her maiden voyage, and after eighty years returned to scheduled passenger service.

Varnished mahogany and wicker seats

(27)

Collection of Steamboat tickets

********* LAKE MINNETONKA STEAMBOATS ** *******

The following list is a compilation of the many steamboats that long ago graced the waters of Lake Minnetonka. Many were built right on the shores of the lake; others were constructed elsewhere or were brought to Minnetonka after service on other lakes. Most were dismantled, burned or sunk, and yet were reborn by having their engines, boilers, bells, whistles or machinery reinstalled in other boats. Many had several names and were often sold, traded or had new owners who rebuilt them, lengthened them, or added new super structures. It was an incredible period of steam transportation that spanned over half a century, and included almost one hundred steamboats before it ended. Alphabetical order. If known: date of first construction /date of last service, other names, misc.

Acte: 1881/1897, formerly named the *Rosander*.
Alert: 1886/1898, small propeller.
Archie: Brought from the Des Moines River in 1880.
Ariel: Brought from the Mississippi River in 1885, formerly the *Mary D.* and *Leona*, later the *Katherine*.
Austin Middleton: 1884 tug, formerly the *Hercules* (1st) and *Katie Lilliger* and earlier built as the *Seventy Six*, (the first tug), later renamed the *Dagmar*.
Belle of Minnetonka: 1882/1892, 300ft. side-wheeler, largest boat ever built at Lake Minnetonka. Capacity of 2500 passengers.
Ben Lennox: 1884/1900, 80ft. renamed the *Manhattan*.
Blixen: circa: 1885, 40ft. propeller previously named the *Minnesota*, *Waseka*, *Me Too*, and the *Twin City*.
Bowman: Circa: 1885, small propeller, also known as the *Woodland*, *Elgin*, *Pickerel* and the *Tribune*.
Caroline: Circa: 1885, small propeller.
Cascade: 1885/1892, propeller.
Casino: 1880s -1900s, formerly *Helena*, *Nellie May* & *Wayzata*..
Charles Edward: 1886/87, 75ft. Sternwheeler.
Chicago: Circa: 1885, small propeller.
City of St. Louis: 1881/99, 160ft. first Lake Minnetonka boat over 100ft. 1st inland vessel in U.S. to be lighted by electricity.
Cleremont: 1880's.
Clyde: 1884, 85ft. formerly named *Ulysses*. (unsuccessful)
Comet: 1897 propeller, frequently cruised to Stubbs Bay.
Como: 1906/1926, 70ft. propeller, Streetcar Boat, TCRT.
Commodore: 1881 supply boat, formerly the *Jeanette*.
Coney Island: 1885 small propeller, formerly the *Maplewood*, nicknamed the *Chugbug*.
Dagmar: 1876/1898, built as the 40ft tug, *Seventy Six*, renamed *Hercules* (1st), *Katie Lilliger*, and the *Austin Middleton*.
Detective: 1886/1887 propeller, (made only one trip).
Detroit: 1884, 65ft. propeller, built as the *Nina*, renamed *Winfield* and the *Fannie L*.
Dot: Circa: 1880's, small propeller.
Elgin: Circa: 1880's, propeller, originally the *Woodland*, also known as the *Bowman*, *Pickerel* and the *Tribune*.
Elmira: 1886 propeller.
Ethel B: 1890's propeller, built as *Geneva*.
Eugene: 1880's, 30ft, propeller, built as *Margaretta*, then *Golden Grain Belt*, then the *Eugene*.
Ewauna: 1900's propeller, renamed *Florence M. Deering*, later *Little Jo*.
Excelsior: 1901/1910, 125ft built as the sternwheeler, *George*.
Fannie L: 1880's propeller, originally the *Nina*, changed to *Winfield*, the *Detroit*, then the *Fannie L*.
Fannie L. Peck: 1884, small propeller, burned at Morse Island, (Big Island).
Florence M. Deering: 1880's, 40ft. propeller also named *Ewauna*, later named *Little Jo*. It had a condensing engine.
Florence I. Wright: 1880's, small propeller.
Flying Dutchman: 1880's, 35ft. later as *Jersey Lily* & *Minnie Cook*.
Forest Queen: 1881 propeller, renamed the *Queen*.
Fresco: 1870's propeller renamed *Why Not*.
Geneva: 1890's propeller later called the *Ethel B*.
George: 1901-10, 125,' sternwheeler, re-named *Excelsior*.
Golden Grain Belt: 1880's, 30ft propeller, previously named *Margaretta*, later the *Eugene*.
Governor Ramsey: 1860, 50ft. side-wheeler, 1st steamboat on Lake Minnetonka, renamed *Lady of the Lake*, then *Minnetonka*.
Grace: 1880's.
Harriet: 1906/1927, 70ft. Streetcar Boat, TCRT.
Hattie May: 1878/1900, 1st sternwheeler, later renamed the *Tonka*.
Hawkeye: 1880 propeller, later named *Reindeer* and *Archie*.
Hebe: 1880, 52ft. propeller, originally named *J.I.C.*
Helena: 1880's propeller, originally named *Nellie May*, later renamed *Wayzata* (2nd), then *Casino*.
Hercules: (1st) 1876/1898, 40ft. tug built as the *Seventy Six* belonging to James J. Hill, rebuilt as the *Katie Lilliger*, then *Austin Middleton*, then the *Dagmar*.
Hercules: (2nd) 1917 tug, built at Excelsior for Twin City Rapid Transit.
Hiawatha: 1876/1887, 78ft. propeller, originally named the *Mary*, rebuilt as the *Hiawatha*, *Star*, then the *Scandinavian*.
Hopkins: 1906/1949, 70ft. Streetcar Boat, renamed Minnetonka in 1927, last steamboat on the lake, scuttled near others, off Big Island in 1949.
Jeanette: 1881, propeller supply boat, re-named *Commodore*.
Jersey Lily: 1885, 35ft. propeller, later named *Flying Dutchman* and then the *Minnie Cook*.
John Alden: 1880's, tug.
Josie Davidson: 1894, 59ft. its engine installed in the *Plymouth*.
Juno: 1880's, propeller launch, built in New York.
Kate: 1876/1899, 45ft, propeller, renamed the *Katie May*, sunk and rebuilt as the *Saucy Kate*, finally burned in 1899.
Katharine: 1885 propeller, from the Mississippi, also named the *Mary D.*, *Leona* and *Ariel*.
Kathleen: 1899 propeller.
Katie Lilligen: 1876/1897 propeller, built as the *Seventy Six*, then named the *Hercules* (1st), renamed the *Austin Middleton*, then *Dagmar*.
Katie May: 1876 propeller, built as the *Kate*, later named *Saucy Kate*.
Kenosha: 1893/1827, 60ft. propeller, renamed the *Victor*.
Kitty: 1889 propeller.
Lady of the Lake: 1869/1873, 50 ft. side-wheeler, originally the *Governor Ramsey*, rebuilt as the *Minnetonka*, then the barge *Mermaid*.
Leon: 1885 propeller.
Leona: 1885 propeller, originally the *Katharine*, also *Mary D.* & *Ariel*.
Little Jo: 1880's/1919, propeller, originally named *Florence M. Deering*, then the *Ewauna*.
Lotos: 1885 propeller, originally the *Phoenix*.
Lotus: 1881/1897, 90ft. propeller, very fast.
Lula: 1884 propeller.
Lulu: 1878, 45ft. propeller, renamed *Nautilus*.
Mabel Lane: 1893, 65ft. propeller, originally *Wildwood*.

Steamboat Puritan - 1901-1914, 85ft double deck propeller Excursion Boat

Manhattan: 1884/1900, 80ft. formerly the *Ben Lennox*.
Maplewood: 1880's, nicknamed *Chugbug*, later as *Coney Island*.
Margaretta: 1890's, 30ft. renamed *Golden Grain Belt*, *Eugene*.
Mary: 1876, 78ft. propeller, rebuilt and renamed *Hiawatha*, then *Scandinavian*, rechristened *Star*, 1887 shipped to Green Bay.
Mary D: 1885, originally *Katharine*, then *Leona* and *Ariel*.
Mayflower: 1898/1914, 70ft. propeller. Excursion boat.
May Queen: 1873/1879, 65ft. Exploded.
Mercury: 1881/1912, 76ft. twin screw, built as *W.D. Washburn*.
Me Too: 1880's/1900, 40ft. propeller, built as the *Minnesota*, renamed *Waseka*, *Twin City*, and *Blixen*.
Miles Standish: 1890's dredge boat.
Milliquata: 1880's, gasoline sternwheeler.
Minneapolis: (1st) 1880/1896, 80ft. propeller.
Minneapolis:(2nd) 1906-1912, 142ft. Big Island ferryboat.
Minnehaha: (1st) 1885, 48ft. propeller.
Minnehaha: (2nd) 1906-26, 70ft. propeller Streetcar Boat.
Minnesota: 1880's/1900, 40ft. propeller, see "*Me Too*."
Minnetonka: (1st) 1860-1873, rebuilt to 58ft. (see *Gov. Ramsey*).
Minnetonka: (2nd) 1906/1912, 142ft. Big Island ferryboat.
Minnetrista: 1869, 28ft. propeller.
Minnie: 1888, propeller.
Minnie Cook: 1880's, 35ft. propeller.
Montcalm: 1886, propeller.
Muskegon: 1900's propeller.
Nautilus: 1878, 45ft. originally named *Lulu*.
Nellie May: 1880's/1906, re-named *Helena*, *Wayzata*, *Casino*.
Nina: 1880's, 65ft. renamed *Winfield*, *Detroit*, & *Fannie L*.
Okoboji: 1900's.
Olga: 1885/1906, propeller, renamed the *Ralph*.
Papoose: 1893/1893, only in service one year, burned.
Patrol: 1886, propeller.
Paul Sherwin: 1890's, propeller.
Phil Sheridan: 1866/1892, 300ft, renamed *Belle of Minnetonka*.
Phoenix: 1885, Propeller, renamed *Lotos*, *Olga* and *Ralph*.
Pickerel: 1880's propeller originally *Woodland*, *Bowman*, *Elgin*, then *Tribune*.
Pilgrim: 1906 propeller, originally the *West Point*.
Plymouth: 1903/1914, 75ft. propeller excursion boat.
Priscilla: 1906, propeller tug boat.
Puritan: 1901/1914, 85ft. double deck propeller.
Ralph: 1885, propeller, originally *Phoenix*, *Lotos*, and *Olga*.
Rambler: 1874/1884, 54ft. sidewheeler.
Reindeer: 1880, propeller, formerly *Hawkeye*, then *Archie*.
Roger Lee: 1905, 35ft. renamed *Frolic*.
Rosander: 1881/1897, propeller, renamed *Acte*.
Rush: 1880's/1895, sidewheeler.
St. Albans: 1880's, propeller.
St. Paul: 1906/1912, 142ft. Big Island ferryboat.
Saucy Kate: 1878/1899, propeller, burned.
Scandinavian: 1876, originally the *Mary*, rebuilt and renamed *Hiawatha*, *Scandinavian* then the *Star*.
Seventy Six: 1876/1898 tug, (see *Hercules* (1st).
Signal: 1880's, 40ft. propeller.
Star: 1876, 78ft. propeller, (see *Mary*).
Stillwater: 1906/1927, 70ft. propeller Streetcar Boat.
Sue Gardiner: 1868, 35ft. 1st propeller on the lake.
Tatu: 1889, first naphtha launch.
Three Friends: 1897, 26ft. propeller.
Tonka: 1878/1900, formerly the sternwheeler *Hattie May*.
Topsy: 1880's private launch renamed *Eagle*.
Tribune: 1885 propeller, see the *Bowman*.
Twin City: 1880's 40ft. propeller, (see *Me Too*).
Ulysses: 1884/1905, 85ft. steel hull, re-named *Clyde*.
Venus: 1889 propeller.
Vergie: 1885, propeller, renamed *West Point*.
Victor: 1893/1927, 60ft. propeller, originally the *Kenosha*.
Waseka: 1880's, 40ft. propeller, (see *Minnesota*).
Wayzata: 1880's, 28ft. propeller, (see *Helena*).
W.D. Washburn: 1881/1912, 76ft. twin screw, re-named *Mercury*.
West Point: 1885, propeller, originally the *Vergie*.
White Bear: 1906/1926, 70ft. propeller Streetcar Boat.
Why Not: 1870's, propeller, originally the *Fresco*.
Wildwood: 1893, 65ft. propeller, renamed *Maple Lane*.
Winfield: 1880's 65ft. (see the *Nina*).
Winnogene: 1890's, propeller.
Woodland: 1885, propeller, (see *Bowman*).
Ypsilanti: 27ft propeller.
Zillah: 1890/1905, propeller, originally *Ulysses*, then *Clyde*.
Zulu: 1880's, small propeller.

BIG ISLAND FERRY

The "*Minneapolis*" was one of three 1000 passenger ferryboats that departed Excelsior every twenty minutes for "Big Island Amusement Park"

The ferrys were 142 ft long, 39ft wide with rudders on both ends for quick turn around. They had three passenger decks and were painted a crisp white to set them apart from the rest of the fleet.

(30)

Excelsior Homeport

Home to over ninety steamboats

Lake Minnetonka

A HISTORICAL INSIGHT

EXCELSIOR

By Jim Ogland, author of
"Picturing Lake Minnetonka"

© DNALGO Enterprises Box 935 Wayzata, Mn 55391

Historic EXCELSIOR

Excelsior's waterfront has always been important and from the very beginning has played a significant role in developing and preserving the historical charm and character of the town. Even today, many of the major excursion and larger charter boats are docked here and consider Excelsior their home port. The recently restored 1906 Steamboat, *Minnehaha,* is also moored here and calls Excelsior home. Pictured on the right, are two prominent turn-of-the-century waterfront structures, **the famous Blue Line Café, and the Casino.**

Thousands of souvenir Minnetonka postcards, such as this one, were printed.

The 1851 signing of the *"Treaties at Mendota and Traverse des Sioux,"* ceding Indian lands West and South of the Mississippi finally opened the way for pioneer settlement of Minnesota. Shortly thereafter, in 1852, Lake Minnetonka was rediscovered by Simon Stevens and Calvin Tuttle. A few months later, in 1853, a colony of New York settlers, led by George Bertram, arrived and chose a site for their village on the southern shores of Lake Minnetonka. **They named their new town "Excelsior."** About 40 members were in the new community. *For a payment of $8, and $1 per wk for a seven month period, each member of the association received a village lot of at least one acre and could also claim 160 acres of land outside the village limits for $1.25 an acre.* Other early arrivals were the Reverend Charles Galpin and Peter Gideon, a fruit grower. Rev. George Galpin built the house (first hotel) in the painting on the right, and his brother Rev. Charles, the first steamboat on the lake.

For hundreds of years, Lake Minnetonka and the land surrounding it had belonged to the Dakota-Sioux Indians and other tribes. It was one of their most favored places in the entire Northwest. Following the treaty signing, much remained to be done before land could be legally claimed: ratification by the U.S. Senate, properly surveyed, and township lines needed to be established.

In an age before the common use of photography, scenes such as the one above were typically captured by watercolorists and artists. One such artist, an Englishman named Edwin Whitefield, painted numerous vistas of Minnetonka. This watercolor entitled *"Excelsior at Lake Minnetonka"* shows the *"Excelsior House"* where Whitefield stayed and painted in 1854.

(34)

PIONEERS an early insight

The following "Preamble" to the "New York Pioneer Association's" constitution and by-laws was adopted November 12, 1852

"PREAMBLE. Whereas, we the undersigned, having associated ourselves into a body to remove to Minnesota Territory next summer {1853), and occupy some of the government lands now vacated by the late treaty with the Sioux Indians, and having been on a tour through the Western states last summer, have selected a site for a village and farming country, that for healthfulness of climate, fertility of soil, beauty of scenery and nearness to markets, cannot be surpassed by any other locality in the country; being within twelve or fifteen miles of two of the most important towns in the territory (St. Paul and St. Anthony Falls) and having a front on a lake, navigable for steam and other boats over forty miles, its waters as clear as crystal and abound with fish. The land around the lake is also supplied with natural meadow, the country is gently rolling and interspersed with the most beautiful growth of sugar maple, black walnut, butternut, white and red oak, and a variety of others; also with wild fruit, grapes and berries of almost every kind. The whole country in fact, possessing almost everything that the heart of man could wish for. Therefore in order to avail ourselves of all the advantages of an old settled country, and secure ourselves such increase of value as must result from a concentration of numbers upon the land, together with our own efforts in its improvement, erection of a village and settling the farms thereupon, and all the blessings of life.. We, each and all of us, who subscribe in the following constitution, do combine ourselves, our means and our energies, in this enterprise and agree to support and carry into effect its laws."

Upon arrival in Minnesota, the Excelsior Association immediately took claim to their 160 acres, which they platted into village lots and the name *Excelsior* was adopted.

Each member would be entitled to a farm, and one village lot of not less than one acre (the farms and lots to be drawn by numbers). Once properties were decided upon, they quickly set about clearing the land and building shelters for their families.

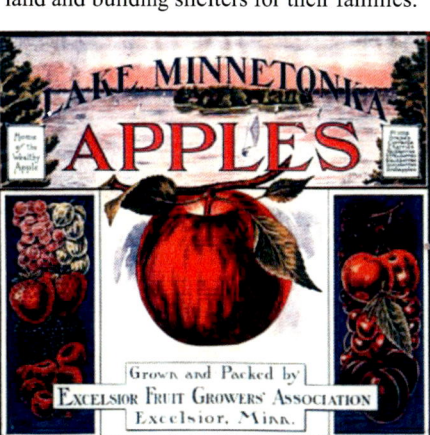

The area's soil was rich and fertile and seemed well suited for growing fruit and vegetables. As a result numerous vineyards, orchards, and farms prospered along the shores. Pioneer, Peter Gideon, claimed 160 acres along what is now Gideons Bay and planted a bushel of apple seeds. It took a few years, but he eventually developed the famous hardy **Wealthy apple**.

Many of the pioneers brought a few packets of precious seeds and vegetables cuttings, flowers and herbs. Locally they found cranberries in the bogs, wild rice and other native plants.

In 1849 Minnesota was organized as a Territory with a population of less than 5000. A few years later and open for settlement, small communities similar to Excelsior were springing up around the lake: Wayzata, Mound, Meadville, Linwood, Deephaven, Tonka Bay, etc. More settlers were coming and thousands more wanted to come. They were people from the New England States who dreamed of getting a new start, of owning their own land. They were immigrants arriving from Germany, Ireland and Scandinavia. **Friendly Sioux Indians still inhabited the area and continued to hunt the plentiful game and gather the rice that grew wild along the shoreline. They did not leave entirely until the Indian uprising of 1862.** As the settlement grew, so did the need for schools, churches, harness shops, blacksmiths, hotels and a doctor. General merchandising and other services would also be needed. **The Reverend Charles Galpin organized the first Congregational Church in 1853.** A log structure Episcopal Church was built in 1862, and a Methodist Society began to hold occasional services.

Chief Shakopee and his band of Indians remained in the area long after the settlers had moved in.

The first school was held in a small log building erected during the summer of 1854. Its first teacher was Miss Jane Wolcott. A larger two-story frame building replaced it in 1857.

Lake Minnetonka and the area surrounding it was undergoing significant change. Land was being cleared, cabins built, roads created and opportunities abounded.

Many colonists came with previous experience and skills. For others it was a new way of life. Building their cabin was an immediate priority, but once completed, subsistence became the main concern. Hezikiah Brake, the treasurer of the colony, set about tapping the vast number of large sugar maples. All spring he tapped and boiled down enough sap to fill several barrels which he then sold for a $200 profit. Other colonists were busy clearing their land, planting vegetables, squash, turnips, corn and potatoes-crops that they could consume or market. Boat trips to the saw mill at Minnetonka Mills brought lumber and supplies. Wood for making boats was acquired as well. **Fishing was good. The fish, mostly bass and pickerel, were plentiful and enough for a week could usually be caught in a few hours.** The colony was becoming a town. Meridian lines had been run, but no government surveys had yet been completed. Farmers had horses, oxen, cattle and even pigs.

An evening row on Lake Minnetonka

In a few short years, the Civil War (1861-1865) will bring even further change to the lake. Tourists and visitors have heard how beautiful and healthful Lake Minnetonka is, and following the war, will arrive in great numbers. They will need lodging, dining and transportation.

TOURISM: Hotels & Steamboats

The new town was rapidly developing as the center of activity on the southern shore. Soon it would become home to merchants, shopkeepers, farmers, hotel operators, steamboat captains and crews. In 1860, the Reverend Charles Galpin of Excelsior, saw the need for a faster way to get from place to place around the densely wooded lake. He hired a carpenter to build a boat and named it the *Governor Ramsey*. It wasn't the most attractive boat, but the fifty foot side-wheeler was soon carrying not only passengers, but mail, food and building supplies to all points on the lake.

*For eight years the **Governor Ramsey** ruled, unchallenged, as the only passenger steamboat on the lake. In 1867, it met the first train at Wayzata, and tourism finally began in earnest.*

In 1868 a rival appeared. The smaller 35ft *Sue Gardiner* had been built in Detroit and unlike the Governor, it had a propeller. This was the first time that a non paddlewheel steamboat was used on the lake. It was purchased by hotel owner, John Mann, and became an important addition to his hotel, the Edgewood.

Following the conclusion of the Civil War and *the coming of the "Iron Age"* not only opened up America's frontier, but within a few short years, would bring fame and fortune to Lake Minnetonka. Visitors and tourists began arriving in great numbers from all over the South. They came from such seemingly far away locations as St. Louis, Memphis, New Orleans, Kansas City and many other southern cities.

They came to escape the suffocating heat of the deep south and to benefit from the cool nights and refreshing climate of Minnesota and especially Lake Minnetonka

THE WHITE HOUSE
C. HOLMDALE & SON,
PROPRIETORS
EXCELSIOR, MINN.
Per day, ... $2.00
Per week, ... $8.00 to $12.00

Residents and entrepreneurs quickly responded to this new and unexpected interest in their lake. Realizing that tourists needed lodging, transportation and dining, they began to provide it.

"The White House Hotel" (1872-1946) in Excelsior was situated in a very prominent position facing the bay at the corner of Lake and Water Streets. It was a landmark and served the community for many years. Its numerous rooms accommodated thirty guests and like most hotels in the area, had a good kitchen as well. Guests relaxed on the large porch and enjoyed the wonderful lake breezes.

Initially Excelsior Township was much larger and included the present cities of Tonka Bay, Shorewood and Greenwood. The original area encompassed the full 36 square miles of a township and included the area north of the narrows. In 1868 this area was taken and added to Medina Township and eventually became the village of Orono.

By the turn of the decade, Lake Minnetonka was becoming an increasingly popular vacation destination.
To accommodate this growing demand, additional hotels and inns were springing up all around the lake. Within the "City" area of Excelsior two popular hotels were the **Sampson House** and the **La Paul Hotel**. The huge Lake Park Hotel at Tonka Bay would soon be built and opened in 1879, as would the Hotel St. Louis and later the Keewaydin Hotel both at Deephaven. They were followed in 1882 by the enormous Hotel Lafayette at Minnetonka Beach.

The 1880's saw a new surge in steam transportation. Railroads brought visitors to the lake and the steamboats provided quick, efficient transportation to the hotels and boarding houses.

The Sampson House
Located in Excelsior, the Sampson House at 500 2nd St. was a popular hotel that survived numerous fires and changes of ownership to become the last survivor of some 20 Excelsior hotels. Finally closing in 1960, it is shown here in its most lasting image (1895).

Smaller hotels, inns and boarding houses sprang up all around the lake. Many started as boarding houses with just a few rooms, but as lodging demands and business prospered, they added on. Some added not only a few rooms, but entire second and even third floors. Often the names of establishments were known as either houses or hotels interchangeably.

One of principal hotels on the lower lake was the **"Keewaydin Hotel."** It was located in Excelsior Township at Cottagewood in Deephaven. Initially known as the *Cottagewood Club House.*

Keewaydin Hotel
With its sturdy dock, the Keewaydin became a regular stop for the new *"Streetcar Boats."* Like so many other hotels it was destroyed by fire in 1924.

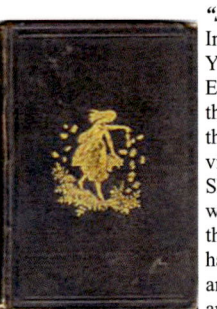

"Summer Rambles in the West"
In 1852 a well known New York writer, Mrs. Elizabeth Ellet, arranged a trip to the then, *Wilds of the West.* Among the many locations that she visited was Lake Minnetonka. She became the first white woman to visit and explore the area. In her published hardcover book, she devotes an entire chapter to Minnetonka and becomes the first woman journalist to visit the lake and write about it. She also named a number of locations, bays and points.

Lake Park Hotel, built in 1879
Originally located in Excelsior Township which later became the Village of Tonka Bay in 1902, the Lake Park Hotel opened as a part of the then popular, Chautaugua movement. After the first year, it changed to a regular hotel and being the largest hotel on the lake, became very popular and renamed the Tonka Bay Hotel.

Hotel La Paul
The Hotel La Paul was the latest of several that had occupied the same site. Beginning as the Galpin House, built in 1854, it was rebuilt in 1870 as the Excelsior House. It became the Hotel La Paul owned by Dr. George La Paul and finally the Excelsior Bay Hotel. Doctor La Paul housed his medical practice at one end of the hotel and also owned and operated the Steamboat *George,* later renamed the *Excelsior.*

A few of the other hotels in Excelsior were: the Mix Hill House on St. Albans Bay, the Beers Hotel, Donaldson House, Maple Inn, Well-Come-Inn, James H. Clark House, DeGroodt's Summer House, the Blueline Hotel, Page's Pleasant Grove House, the Appledore, Fred Hawkins Hotel, and the Long View House.

The lake was soon dotted with hotels. Many of them were just summer places and often had cottages as well. **Most were built between the 1850's and 1890's.** Many of these and other hotels often acquired new ownership and new names.

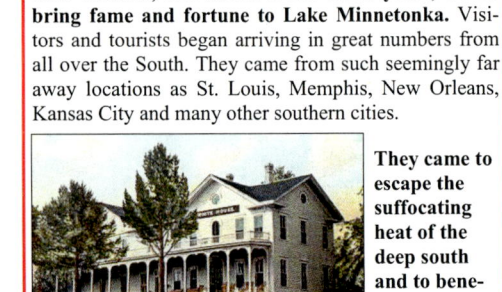

(36)

EXCELSIOR: Home Port

Many of the smaller hotels had their own steamboats. Most however, did not. They relied instead on the lake steamers to bring arriving guests from the train stations to their hotels. In addition to carrying arriving and departing passengers, the steamers delivered building materials and other supplies to locations all around the lake. **Over the years countless boats of all descriptions have made Excelsior their home port.** This included the 2500 passenger *"Belle of Minnetonka,"* and the 160 foot, *"City of St. Louis."* The sternwheeler excursion boat, *Excelsior,* along with the propellers *Puritan, Plymouth,* and *Mayflower* were also here.

Prominent structures marking the waterfront, were the **Blue Line Café and the Casino.** It was here that the often bustling crowds would arrive for lunch, for a snack or like today, *to just be part of the scene.* The waterfront and boats were what people wanted. Excursion boats were busy, rental rowboats were popular, the fast express boats were exciting, cute and fun to ride. Steamers took them to their hotels.

The large white boats in the background are the three new Big Island Ferryboats. Rental row boats are at the bottom of the photo.

300ft "Belle of Minnetonka" docked in Excelsior

Sternwheeler Excursion Boat, *Excelsior*

The **Port of Excelsior** had numerous docks which stretched all along the shore line. The larger boats were docked in front of and to the east of the Blue Line Café, which was located on the shore at the foot of Water Street. Smaller craft were moored in the other direction. **Many hotels around the lake had their own dock and boats located here,** and were used to transport arriving guests to their hotels.

Several smaller launches can be seen in the foreground. Most are steam powered, but newer "gas engine" propellers are beginning to appear. Soon steam will be a thing of the past

When the Big Island Amusement Park opened in 1906, the TCRT built three one thousand passenger ferryboats to transport patrons to the island. **The Excelsior docks were their home port.** On weekends and holidays a ferry left Excelsior for the Island every twenty minutes. They were painted white to distinguish them from the rest of the Twin City Rapid Transit Company fleet and were named the *Minneapolis,* the *St. Paul* and the *Minnetonka.* They were 142ft long and double ended, meaning they could go in either direction without turning around. Surprisingly fast, they made the round trip to Big Island in approximately fifty minutes.

Steamboats and Lake Minnetonka have been important to each other. From the very first one, the *Governor Ramsey,* built in 1860, to the very last one, the *Minnetonka,* sunk in 1949, there has been a bond between the two. Over ninety steamboats have plied the waters of Minnetonka. Some were huge and luxurious, others were more functional. Most or all of them have at one time or another docked at the Excelsior Docks. It was an incredible period.

Approaching the Excelsior docks after racing across the lake from Wayzata are the *City of St. Louis, Lotus,* and the giant *Belle of Minnetonka.*

(37)

The GOLDEN YEARS 1900 - 1930

The *Glory Years* (1880's-1890's) were over. **Minnetonka was sleeping.** The big hotels, the huge steamboats, the summer residents from the East and the South were all gone. **The same trains that had brought them here were now taking them to Yellowstone, Glacier, and the seaside resorts of the East coast.** The Victorian Period was ending and Lake Minnetonka had been more or less forgotten as a tourist attraction.

But not for long. Thomas Lowry president of the Twin City Rapid Transit Company began to change all that. Lowry was a visionary who saw Lake Minnetonka as a natural recreational area. He saw it as perhaps unique in all of America - a beautiful blue freshwater lake with over one hundred miles of shoreline, teeming with fish, close to the large cities of Minneapolis and St. Paul and a population anxious to spend their new found prosperity.

Lowry and the sprawling streetcar company recognized the need to develop destination points for people to visit *and to give them some reason to ride his streetcars.* Embarking on an incredibly ambitious plan, Lowry purchased the huge Tonka Bay Hotel, bought 65 acres on Big Island (on which to build an amusement park), ordered the construction of six fast streetcar-like express boats, extended his streetcar line to Excelsior and Deephaven, and purchased all the remaining excursion and passenger steamboats on the lake. He further commissioned the construction of three 142ft one thousand passenger ferry boats; all of this to be completed and ready for the 1907 summer season.

In the spring of 1905, residents of Excelsior awoke to the pounding of spikes. Tracks were being laid on Water Street and soon to follow were bright yellow double-decker streetcars.

A new kind of tourist was waiting to come. The new tourist would visit the lake just for the day. They came from the nearby cities and towns. They came to ride the excursion boats and the new torpedo stern "Express Boats." They rode the fast yellow streetcars to Excelsior, then boarded the 1000 passenger ferryboats to Big Island. There were excursion boats to ride, picnics and band concerts, and rowboats to rent.

This is a typical "early bird" Minnetonka fisherman special that departed every morning at 4:30am for the lake. It is pictured in front of the downtown ticket office at 17 N 6th Street in Minneapolis.

In the summer of 1905, streetcars began rolling westward to Lake Minnetonka. With them came excited tourists and first time visitors to the lake looking for summer fun. Riding the streetcars to Minnetonka was in itself quite an experience, as they often reached mile-a-minute speeds and wobbled from side to side. As many as sixty streetcars were on the tracks at the same time coming and going to Lake Minnetonka.

The Great White Way. .
By day it was named the route of greenery and scenery. At night it was the *Great White Way,* so called, because of the spectacular way in which it was illuminated. It made night trips very unique and created a memory that lasted forever.

The roomy cars accommodated 48 passengers and made the trip to Excelsior in 50 minutes.

BIG ISLAND AMUSEMENT PARK

Big Island was built as a destination location to increase streetcar ridership to Excelsior. It was basically a picnic park, but had numerous amusement rides to make it a fun time. **Its focal point was the spectacular 200ft tower created to resemble the famous tower of Seville in Spain. At night its brilliant beacon helped to guide the three huge passenger ferryboats to and from the park and the periodic weekend band concerts.** Concerts were held in the parks main attraction, the "Music Casino," with seating for over 1500 comfortably. The bands stayed at local hotels and boarding houses in Excelsior and therefore residents became acquainted with individual band members and some even got musical instruction from them. It was a period of prosperity for all.

SIX FAST 130 PASSENGER EXPRESS BOATS

Six streetcar boats were built to compliment and extend the Excelsior streetcar line. A seventh boat, the *"Excelsior"* was built in 1915. They were colorful, popular, and soon became the darlings of the lake. They docked in Excelsior and daily made 27 stops on four different routes in both the upper and lower lake. The fare between any two points was only 10 cents. They ran in good weather or bad for over twenty years.

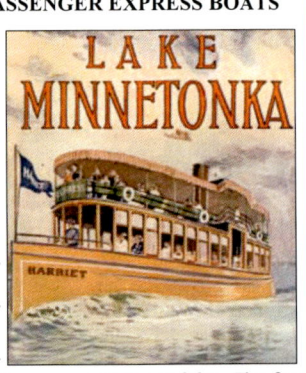

(38)

ROARING TWENTIES

BIG ISLAND PARK CLOSES

At the end of the 1911 season the Big Island Amusement Park closed for good. Henry Ford's Model T and other new-fangled automobiles gave people the opportunity to go elsewhere and attendance at the park had dropped way off. TCRT also closed the Tonka Bay Hotel, dismantled the ferryboats and sold the excursion boats.

In 1920 Horace Lowry, president of the Twin City Rapid Transit line, offered the Tonka Bay pavilion (roller skating rink) to the City of Excelsior. It was dismantled, reassembled in Excelsior and became the largest dance hall in the Midwest. It could accommodate over 2000 dancers and was sometimes used as a roller rink. Towards the end of the twenties it was sold to park owner Fred Pearce and **later became Big Reggie's Danceland.** It closed for good in 1968. Pearce further expanded the park by purchasing the Blue Line Café and the lakeshore in between. He also bought the adjacent picturesque Wyer house.

AMUSEMENT PARK IN EXCELSIOR

In 1924, Fred Pearce of Detroit, proposed building a new amusement park on the grounds of the former streetcar and Express Boat Dock Station property. The new park opened with celebration on Memorial Day, May 30, 1925. One of the most popular rides was the 65ft high roller coaster which contained over one half mile of track. The "merry-go-round," enclosed in a circular building, was also a favorite.

The park was large, covered many acres, and had numerous rides, that included the ferris wheel, dodgem cars, tilta-whirl, the whip, a miniature train, the caterpillar and other features such as the funhouse.

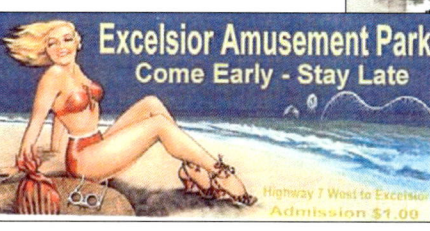

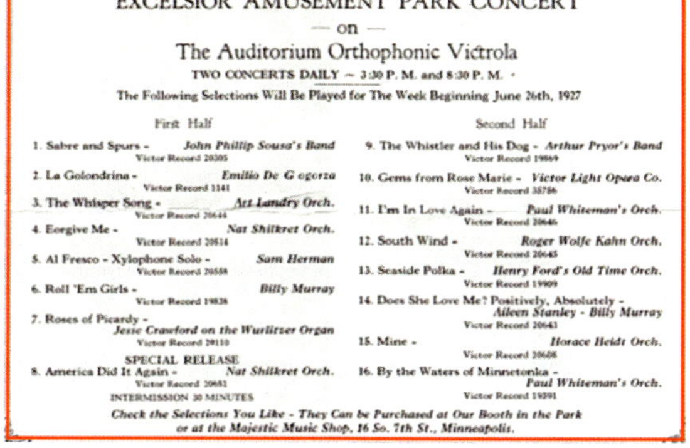

The **"Roaring Twenties"**... were like no other time in American history. They brought the flappers, raccoon coats, spats and prohibition. The times were wild, they were fun! They ushered in a new era, an era that brought more changes and challenges to Lake Minnetonka.

By the late-twenties Excelsior had become a household word. Visits to the park had become an exciting event for organizations, individuals, and groups of all ages. Eventually to increase attendance, the park added free attractions, such as live concerts, circus acts, and even daredevil events. Miss Minnesota contests and celebrations of all kinds were held at the park. A chance to be on the water was provided by "around the bay rides" in fast mahogany Chris Craft boats. It was a thrilling and exciting experience for many visitors and inner-city dwellers.

The automobile had arrived! In the 1920's ordinary people became less dependent on public transportation. With the coming of the automobile came the construction of better roads. People traveled faster and further and soon discovered new places to visit. Ridership on the streetcars and boats began to diminish. Despite the fascination with the new automobiles, and the mobility that they provided, hundreds of visitors still came every weekend to Excelsior and Lake Minnetonka. They came to fish or to just enjoy being near the water. During the week, the growing resident population of Excelsior rode the train or streetcars to work in the Twin Cities. As the years went by, the lake continued to attract more and more residents. Summer cottages became year around homes and the larger towns built new schools and churches to accommodate the increasing population. **Like each preceding decade, the roaring twenties brought new changes to Lake Minnetonka.** Chief among them was the drawing to a close of the streetcar/steamboat era. It was the end of a fabulous period.

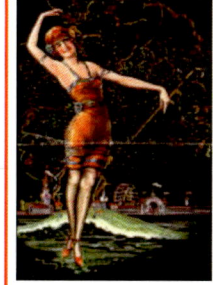

This was the program cover for a Victrola concert at the Park

By 1926 ridership on the onetime indispensable fleet of fast, yellow Express Boats, had fallen way off. This decline in boat patronage at first resulted in reduced schedules; then one by one the boats were withdrawn, until finally service was stopped altogether. In July of 1926 three boats, the *Como*, *Whitebear* and the *Minnehaha* were sunk in deep water off Big Island. The *Hopkins* was sold and used as a excursion boat until 1949. *Harriet*, *Stillwater* and *Excelsior* were dismantled.

Swimming and diving at the Excelsior beach

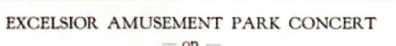

(39)

LAKE MINNETONKA APPLES

Home of the Wealthy Apple

Plums
Grapes
Currants
Cherries
Raspberries
Strawberries
Blackberries
Gooseberries
Crabapples

Grown and Packed by
EXCELSIOR FRUIT GROWERS' ASSOCIATION
Excelsior, Minn.

The increasing number of fruit farmers along the Excelsior side of Lake Minnetonka's southern shores soon led to the formation of the *"Excelsior Fruit Growers' Association."* During the fruit growing season producers brought their products to Excelsior for local purchase or shipment to market areas. Among the principal fruits grown were strawberries, blackberries, gooseberries, raspberries, apples, cherries, grapes and plums. This became a sizeable operation and eventually led to the opening of a canning factory enabling customers to have Minnetonka's choicest products on the table the year around.

Wayzata

The Gilded Age, 1866 - 1920

Lake Minnetonka

A HISTORICAL INSIGHT

WAYZATA

By Jim Ogland, author of
"Picturing Lake Minnetonka"

© DNALGO Enterprises Box 935 Wayzata, Mn 55391

(43)

WAYZATA

A HISTORICAL LOOK AT EARLY WAYZATA, ITS ENVIRONS AND ITS PEOPLE

The early Sioux Indians, that lived along Minnetonka's northern shore called it "*Waziya,*" *the northern god, a giant who blew the cold winds of the north from his mouth.* It was here that they hunted, fished, harvested the wild rice and picked seasonal berries. The 1851, signing of the Traverse des Sioux Treaty with the Indians, allowed settlement of additional Minnesota territory including the lands around Lake Minnetonka. Among the first pioneers to arrive in 1852 was Oscar E. Garrison, a visionary, who immediately recognized the location along the shore as the ideal spot for a new town. With its commanding view of the lower lake and cooling southern breezes, it was the perfect site. Across the Bay, on a narrow point, a large earthen mound, was readily visible. The local Indian bands called it *Spirit Knob,* and it was very significant to the spiritual life of the Dakota. Ceremonies, medicine rites and festivals were frequently held here. Much later the knob was leveled and the location re-named Breezy Point.

Spirit Knob

Spirit Knob in the distance viewed from near City Hall

HOMESTEAD
Settlers were entitled to stake a claim for 160 acres. Opportunity to own your own land. Requirements: One had to clear an acre, build a 8x10 floored dwelling with a door & window, have it surveyed and witnessed, pay the government $1.25 an acre.

Arriving at the lake in June of 1852, Wayzata's first pioneer settler, Oscar E. Garrison, staked out a claim and built a log cabin shanty located on what is now Lake Street, between Broadway and Walker. The area around the lake, which eventually became known as the Big Woods, was covered with very heavy brush and timber. Together with another early settler named Alfred B. Robinson, they cleared a pathway, wide enough for oxen-teams to St. Anthony (later named Minneapolis).

All during the summer and fall of 1854, Garrison and Robinson teamed up to lay-out and survey the new town site of Wayzata. The site plan and plat could not be submitted until completion by government surveyors of area township and subdivision lines. In the spring of 1855, a Certificate of Dedication of the plat of Wayzata, signed by Oscar Garrison and Lucius Walker, was filed and recorded with the Register of Deeds at the Hennepin County Land Office. **Wayzata was now on the map!**

During the summer of 1854, Garrison hired Amos Gray to help build the first, much needed general store and the first steam-powered sawmill in Wayzata. The sawmill created a number of new jobs and provided lumber for the building of new dwellings and business structures.

The cholera death of a new arrival in 1855 was Wayzata's first death and its first burial. The young man was interred in the cemetery located at Walker Ave. and Wayzata Blvd.

1855: A stagecoach operation from Wayzata to St. Paul, through Minneapolis, was initiated by entrepreneurs Lucius C. Walker and Oscar Garrison. The stage left early each Monday, Wednesday, and Friday morning for Minneapolis and returned to Wayzata on Tuesday, Thursday and Saturdays. The twenty-five mile trip took about five hours. **This was probably the start of the first opportunity for tourists to visit Lake Minnetonka, and it prompted the need for hotels and dining rooms to accommodate visitors.**

Garrison saw the need for many things and set about accomplishing them. He petitioned the District Court for a road to Wayzata from the Mississippi River, and one from Bassett's Creek, and later a road to Wayzata from nearby Minnetonka Mills. This was McGinty Road.

1903 map of Wayzata Bay

With the newly acquired Indian lands, Lake Minnetonka was now open for settlement. It did not take long for eager pioneers to begin trickling in. First one family and then another. Home sites in and around Wayzata were soon claimed. Larger tracts of land were sometimes obtained when chosen next to each other by brothers or other family kin. If for example, a family member claimed 160 acres and another family member claimed an adjacent 160 acre parcel, together they would own 320 acres. As the settlements grew, so did the need for schools, churches, harness shops, blacksmiths, hotels and a doctor if they were lucky. Enterprising pioneers realized these needs and soon provided them.

The first post office in the area was established in the village of Minnetonka in 1855 with the second post office located at Wayzata in the same year.

(44)

Pioneers - Settlers

Pioneer living was certainly not for everyone, but for many families it was the chance for a new beginning, a new life. Initially they came from the Eastern United States, New York, Pennsylvania, Ohio, etc. Eventually they came from Europe, far away from their native countries, mostly from Germany and Scandinavia. They were hardy souls, willing to endure numerous hardships. Along with the major task of clearing their new lands, they struggled against the cold Minnesota winters. Finally in 1857 with crops in place, and expectations high, a new challenge appeared - grasshoppers! They devoured everything in sight. *Times were tough and some settlers considered giving up, but miraculously "ginseng" was discovered growing wild in the woods. The Chinese were willing to pay handsomely for this strange medicinal root and profits from its sale provided enough income to see many a settler through the hard times. For a few years Minnesota exported over 200,000 pounds of ginseng annually.*

The Great Seal of the State of Minnesota

On May 11, 1858, Minnesota became the 32nd State admitted to the Union. The seal is also found on the state flag. It depicts a farmer plowing on the banks of the Mississippi River with his gun and powder horn within reach. The state motto is at the top of the flag in French.. "L'Etoile du Nord"- **Star of the North.**

Up until now, log cabins had been the norm. With logs readily available from the land as it was being cleared, they were quick and easy to build. Most were small, met the requirements of a claim shanty, and provided temporary shelter. Once the homestead claim was completed and ownership established, settlers began to build more permanent homes and buildings. Sawmills provided lumber, siding, shakes and shingles. Before long, the town of Wayzata was beginning to take shape.

With more and more arriving settlers, workers and guests, the need for lodging was becoming a necessity. The first hotel at the lake was built next to the sawmill at Minnetonka Mills in 1853 by Stevens and Tuttle.

Soon thereafter, William Harrington filed a claim for 160 acres on Lookout Point on the Ferndale peninsula. His brother, John Harrington, claimed an adjacent quarter section and began construction of a large farmhouse which he named "Lake Side Home." He soon added 16 rooms and changed the name to **Harrington Inn,** and in 1854, became Wayzata's first hotel. The second hotel was the **Day's Inn** built by Abel Day, Wayzata's first postmaster, and his wife, Eliza. It was of rudimentary log construction and primarily accommodated claim seekers. **Two more hotels came along in the 1850's.** Wm Dudley, a local blacksmith, built an upscale hotel, **Dudley's,** on Lake Street at Walker Ave. It featured charming quarters with clean beds. Also on Lake St., at the corner of Lake and Broadway, was the half-log, half-frame, **Keesling Hotel.** This was downtown Wayzata in 1857: A sometimes muddy street, three hotels, a blacksmith shop, a livery and a small general store.

Chief Shakopee, (Little Six, so called by the whites because Shakopee translated means six and he was little in size). **He and his band camped for years along the northern shore near the present site of Wayzata.** Another Indian band also camped along the peninsula between Wayzata Bay and Grays Bay. Each spring they departed for Ta-tonka-ka-gapi, the home of the buffalo, for their summer and fall hunts. They returned to the winter camp laden with buffalo meat, jerked, (thin strips cured in the sun) or sacked in hides for making pemmican (similar to dried beef).

Wayzata's first school house was a log cabin, built in 1858, approximately where Redeemer Lutheran Church is located today. The new Wayzata School District 52 was organized to include Minnetonka, Plymouth, Orono and Medina. Orono was still at that time part of Excelsior township.

Civil War: 1861-1865 On January 9, 1861, Governor Alexander Ramsey delivered his annual message to the Minnesota state legislature and warned of the gathering clouds of war. South Carolina had just seceded and more southern states were likely to follow. In early April, while in Washington, Ramsey heard of the firing on Fort Sumter. He rushed to the war department and offered a thousand Minnesota volunteers for the Union cause. Nine young men from Wayzata volunteered and served bravely in the Union army. Eventually, over twenty three thousand Minnesota men served during the Civil war.

The First Minnesota Regiment was involved in numerous battles and skirmishes throughout the Civil War. They served with gallantry and honor at Bull Run, Fredericksburg, Chancellorsville and Gettysburg. The Third Minnesota Regiment made up of about 400 Minnesota volunteers was involved in the siege and capture of the Confederate stronghold at Vicksburg, There is a large Minnesota memorial at the Vicksburg National Cemetery honoring those that fought and died there.

The first steamboat arrived at the Wayzata docks in the year 1860. It was built by a ship's carpenter for the Reverend Charles Galpin of Excelsior and was named the *"Governor Ramsey."* It provided the first transportation on the lake and was soon carrying not only passengers, but mail, and supplies to Excelsior, Mound and all points on the lake.

Sioux Indian Uprising: 1862 Rebelling against poor treatment and unkept government promises, the Sioux Indians attacked and killed settlers all along the Minnesota River. Fearing for their lives, Minnetonka pioneers fled to the safety of Fort Snelling. Others boarded boats to Big Island. Local men volunteered to help put down the Indian uprising.

1865: At the end of the Civil War, the lake area was still more or less a wilderness. Development and growth had been put on hold during the war, but now with the soldiers returning, a renewed and invigorated spirit was beginning to immerge.

The coming of the "Iron Age"
The first locomotive to the lake arrived in Wayzata on August 24, 1867, and with it, ushered in an entirely new era. The tracks that had been completed only the day before would now bring prosperity and a train once a day to Wayzata. Visitors soon began arriving daily. They came to see beautiful Minnetonka and the new town that was taking its place at the head of the lake. Wealthy southerners had heard about the cool, scenic, and healthful lake and were anxious to escape the heat of the summer south.

The steam engine "William Crooks" made a round trip from Minneapolis to Wayzata once each day.

The "Wayzata Theater Marquee" 1932—1985

Minnesota Historical Society Photo

James J. Hill and the Great Northern Railroad

(46)

RAILROADS, BOATS & RESORTS

IN THE LATE SUMMER OF 1867 the railroad and a new era arrived in Wayzata.
All week residents had watched the laying of rails along the lakeshore in downtown Wayzata. On this sultry morning of August 24th, they were awakened by the excited whistle of the first train to arrive at Lake Minnetonka. The coming of the "Iron Age" not only opened up the American frontier, but within a few short years, would bring fame and fortune to Lake Minnetonka.

The Wm Crooks was the first locomotive in Minnesota. It made daily trips to Wayzata and was turned around on a horse drawn turntable.

"All Aboard." Soon visitors and tourists alike began arriving in great numbers from all over the south. They came from such seemingly faraway locations as St. Louis, Memphis, New Orleans, Kansas City, and many other southern cities. They came to escape the suffocating heat of the deep south and to benefit from the cool nights and refreshing climate of Minnesota and especially Lake Minnetonka.

Aided by the railroad that had begun promoting "Minnetonka" as a famous summer resort, residents and entrepreneurs quickly responded to this new and unexpected interest in their lake. They realized that tourists needed lodging, transportation and dining and they began to provide it.

James J. Hill, the Empire Builder, became a legendary and often controversial figure. Beginning as a clerk, he rose to eventually become the president and owner of perhaps the greatest railroad in the Northwest.

James J. Hill, about 1910

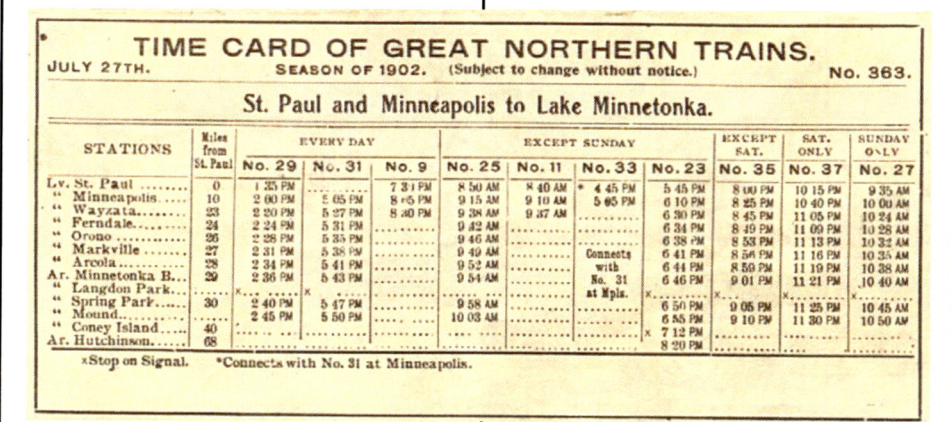

In 1893, Hill drove the final spike commemorating the completion of the transcontinental railroad. Once referred to as "Hill's Folly," it was a momentous achievement.

Hill and Wayzata . . . . .
He had a long standing feud with the city of Wayzata because he had located the tracks along the water front. For spite, he moved the depot to the edge of town. In 1906 Hill finally relented and built what has been described as the best looking depot on the entire line. It remains today as a Wayzata landmark and a wonderful reminder of those halcyon days at the turn of the century.

Pictured at the Wayzata docks in 1881 are the Hattie May, Minneapolis, Lotus and City of St. Louis.

To see the boats lined up at the Wayzata docks awaiting the trains, blowing their whistles in anticipation, was a sight to behold. Families from the South arrived with what seemed like endless quantities of luggage and servants. Wayzata was the first stop. They came for the summer and they came for a good time!

It was an incredible era of steam transportation and the beginning of the "Glory Years" at Lake Minnetonka!

It was the dawn of an exciting, wonderful and marvelous period.

The 165ft steamboat, "The City of St. Louis" in Wayzata Bay

With the rail connection, now at Wayzata, transportation to and from the growing number of hotels was much needed. **Steamboats were the answer.** Initially many individual hotels acquired their own small steamers. The Edgewood Hotel had the 35ft *Sue Gardiner*, the 28ft *Minnetrista* was launched in 1869, and Charles Burwell had the *Fresco*. As the hotels grew in number and size, larger and larger boats appeared on the lake. Some were built as passenger boats and delivered travelers from the Wayzata station to various hotels; others were primarily excursion or sight-seeing boats. The huge 165ft *"City of St. Louis,"* was launched at Wayzata on June 4, 1881. Not to be outdone, J.J. Hill built the enormous 300ft, 2500 passenger *"Belle of Minnetonka"* on the shore at Wayzata. It was the largest steamboat ever built at Minnetonka.

(47)

THE GILDED AGE   1866 - 1920

The "Gilded Age" is generally described by historians as the incredible period between 1866 and 1920. Following the Civil War (1865), it was a time of rapid industrial growth, which produced a new "leisure class" with the time and resources to enjoy for the first time, their new found wealth. Many of them looked to Lake Minnetonka and Wayzata as a place to vacation and pursue leisure activities, such as fishing, sailing, cycling, golf, tennis, etc.

Frank H. Peavey's Ferndale summer home, Highcroft, 1904

Much like Michigan's Mackinac Island, wealthy families began to build palatial "summer homes" at Ferndale and along Bushaway road.

Summer cottage of W.G. Northrup, 1904

By the turn of the century additional huge mansions had been built along the Wayzata shoreline. Many were owned by prominent members of the areas growing milling and lumbering industries.

THE GLORY YEARS

The 1880's, and 90's were, without a doubt, Lake Minnetonka's finest hour. This was the resort period, a time of the enormous steamboats and the huge hotels.

Beginning in 1870, many hotels sprang up all around the lake. Some of these were the first real tourist hotels. Included were the **Gleason and Minnetonka Houses** in Wayzata. The Gleason House at Walker and Lake St. operated for almost 100 years, finally closing in 1964. The Minnetonka was located at Broadway and Lake Street and its 50 rooms could accommodate 100 guests. It had its own dock and rental boats.

Another popular, and the largest of the Wayzata Hotels, was the **Arlington Hotel** built in 1880. It was a three story structure with over 100 rooms. Reportedly J.J. Hill purchased it in 1882 and closed it for good to eliminate it as competition for his soon to open Lafayette Hotel at Mtka Beach. Opening in 1901, the **Northland Inn** was one of Wayzata's last hotels to open. It was located near the Holdridge station on the east end of town. With its electric lights, hot baths, and several cottages, it was a popular spot.

Waiting on the Wayzata dock for an excursion boat

At the end of the 1870's, Lake Minnetonka, noted for its cool nights and pleasant summer days, was fast becoming the resort place to visit. **More accommodations were, however, still needed.** As the decade ended, the Hotel St. Louis opened at Deephaven with 200 rooms, each with a veranda overlooking the lake. Opening the same year (1879) at Tonka Bay was the 1000 guest, Lake Park Hotel.

In 1886 over 10,000 guests had registered at the Hotel St. Louis, Lake Park and the Lafayette Hotel. As many as 2500 visitors were reportedly visiting Lake Minnetonka each day.

The "Belle of Minnetonka" shown here, had a full band on board wherever it went. Each day it met the morning train at Wayzata, then raced the "City of St. Louis" across the six miles of open water to Excelsior. The *Belle* being the larger and faster of the two boats usually won.

The gigantic Hotel Lafayette

Not to be out-done, James J. Hill built the huge 800ft Hotel Lafayette at Minnetonka Beach. It opened on Sunday, July 2, 1882, with great pomp and celebration. All 300 rooms were filled. As a major train stop along the way, this of course brought more and more visitors to Wayzata.

Sailboats were always popular and important. The *Minnetonka Yacht Club* was formed in 1882 with George Brackett as its first Commodore. Early races and regattas began off Orono Point and later at Lookout Point.

In the 1890's a bicycle craze swept across the nation. Everyone was riding bicycles! Wayzata was no exception. Both men and women, enjoyed this new-found and exciting freedom. Some, like W.H. Bovey, pictured here in 1895, rode an elegant "high wheel."

Cycling

(48)

TURN OF THE CENTURY

By 1890, the incredible *Glory Days* of the 1880's at Lake Minnetonka were coming to a close. The *Belle of Minnetonka* remained tied to the dock for the entire 1892 season. **Minnetonka's prosperous resort days were over!** The expansion of the transcontinental railroad system and the extensive promotion of the new national parks seemed exciting. **The wealthy southern tourists were going elsewhere** and the lake was bypassed as a tourist destination.

A NEW ERA

Minnetonka and Wayzata were sleeping, but not for long. Suddenly in 1906, Thomas Lowry and his Twin City Rapid Transit Company announced plans to build an amusement park on Big Island, build three 1000 passenger ferry boats and launch six, fast, streetcar express boats. In addition, J.J. Hill built a spectacular new train depot in downtown Wayzata, said to be the best looking depot on the Great Northern Line.

A fleet of seven all-weather boats, provided fast, dependable, daily, on-time service, to all points on the upper and lower lake.

Streetcars on the lake!

The exciting new boats were unique, unusual and eye-catching with their torpedo sterns, bright yellow color, upper deck benches, cane seats, sharp bows and streetcar-like appearance. **They were designed in Wayzata by Royal Moore of the Moore Boat Works.** Many of the heavy timbers, ribs, frames etc. were sawn at the Wayzata yard and transported to the streetcar barn in Minneapolis where they were built.

They operated successfully for the next twenty years, but times changed and by 1926 service was discontinued. The boats were dismantled or sunk in deep water off Big Island.

BOAT BUILDING

Boat building was an important industry during the first part of the new century. Located along the Wayzata shoreline were the Moore Boat Works, (next to the depot) the Wise Boat Works, (approximately where the Wayzata Yacht Club is now) and the Swaggert Boat Works on Lake St. As gasoline engines developed, W.H. Campbell Co., also located in Wayzata, made marine engines. The Moore Boat Works became the Ramaley Boat Works in about 1910 and continued to build fine boats until the Minnetonka Boat Works was formed in 1929, with a merger of several local boat works. For years they built a line of fine cedar strip "Tonka Craft" fishing boats. They also became one of the world's largest Chris Craft dealers.

The arrival of the automobile brought major change to Wayzata. Prior to 1900, few working class residents owned their own homes. They rented or boarded with others. Now with the ability to own an automobile, they could live at the lake and easily commute to Minneapolis or St. Paul. This meant better job opportunities and more income. It also resulted in better roads. Highway 12 to Minneapolis was established along with other improved and paved roadways. Gas stations and auto dealerships sprang up on Lake Street. Rettinger Ford began selling Model T's in 1913. Dickey and Martinson's Station opened in 1914; others soon followed.

An additional commuter connection to Minneapolis was established in 1914 with the arrival of the first electric Luce Line trolley. The Line arrived on the northern edge of Wayzata and continued on to Stubbs Bay, then to Hutchinson. It was financially unsuccessful and lasted only a few years. The roadbed today is a popular trail.

Supporters meet the first Luce Line trolley

By 1917 there were enough commuters to Minneapolis to warrant a bus operation. Mr. Hart DuPrey of Wayzata created the first bus by extending the frame of a White touring car and adding a bus body. Later Mack truck frames were used and eventually buses were being manufactured in the Minnetonka Boat Works facility. This was the beginning of the Greyhound Bus Company.

Throughout the twenties the lake continued to be the center of numerous activities. Sailboat races, motorboat racing, fishing and swimming were all very popular. Locals from the surrounding areas came to be part of it.

Ferndale shore with Spirit Island in the distance

The **"ROARING TWENTIES"** were like no other time in American history. They brought the Charleston, the flappers, raccoon coats, spats and prohibition. It was a wonderful time! F. Scott Fitzgerald lived and wrote in St. Paul, women received the right to vote and **Wayzata got a new High School.** The Pueblo-styled school opened in September of 1921 with 22 seniors in its first graduating class. Located on the top of the hill at Rice and Broadway, it was Wayzata's only public school for the next thirty years. It was later named Widsten School for Principal Halvor Widsten.

A *"stately"* new City Hall was built in 1904 on the corner of Lake and Manitoba. As an all purpose building, it not only housed the town library, but the jail, and fire fighting equipment as well. Like so many other Wayzata buildings, it burnt to the ground in 1955.

NUMEROUS DAIRY FARMS once operated in and around Wayzata. Ferndale and Highcroft was home to huge palatial homes. It was also home to prize winning dairy cows. At least six local farms had dairy herds and produced milk every day. Bowman's farm was located in the 1920's where the Wayzata Country Club is located today and had 50 Golden Guernseys. Other Wayzata dairy farms were located in the Highlands, Hollybrook, Ferndale North and Holdridge. Several other farms were located around the lake.

Wayzata and Lake Minnetonka have witnessed many changes since those first pioneer settlers arrived on its shores so long ago. Gone are the idyllic, carefree days of summer, gone are the rowboats, the band concerts, the big hotels and the sounds of steamboats. Gone are the passenger trains, the white dresses, parasols, huge hats, wool swimming suits, iced tea and Sunday socials.

Souvenir Books

These small, hard cover, picture books were very popular souvenirs for Lake Minnetonka tourists

(49)

No. 12125

"By the Waters of Minnetonka"
An Indian Love Song

J. M. CAVANASS

Andante moderato

THURLOW LIEURANCE

BY THE WATERS OF MINNETONKA

AN INDIAN LOVE SONG

BY

THURLOW LIEURANCE

+12125 LOW VOICE, WITH VIOLIN AND FLUTE AD LIB...60
+14561 HIGH VOICE, WITH VIOLIN AND FLUTE AD LIB...60
+12927 PIANO SOLO........................40
+15218 VIOLIN & PIANO....................75

Philadelphia
Theodore Presser Co.
1712 Chestnut Str

Yachting

Most famous Lake in the Northwest

Lake Minnetonka

A HISTORICAL INSIGHT

YACHTING

By Jim Ogland, author of
"Picturing Lake Minnetonka"

DNALGO Box 935 Wayzata, Mn

YACHTING...TIME LINE

1680s Early trappers refer to Minnetonka as *"lac gros"* in the *"grand bois,"* "Big lake in the woods." Indians keep the lake a secret.

1822 Two young boys from Ft Snelling paddle up Minnehaha Creek and ***discover*** Lake Minnetonka. It remains a secret for the next thirty years.

1851 Important "Traverse de Sioux and Mendota Treaties" are **signed with Indians,** opening way for area pioneer settlement.

1852 Simon Stevens and Calvin Tuttle rediscover Lake Minnetonka, build dam and sawmill at Minnetonka Mills. Governor Alexander Ramsey visits lake. After learning that Indians call it "Min-ni-tan-ka," he officially names it Minnetonka.

1853 First hotel in lake area opened, located at Minnetonka Mills. Pioneer Association headed by George Bertram, arrives from New York and settles Excelsior.

1858 Minnesota admitted to the Union. Becomes the 32nd state on May 11, 1858.

1860 Rev. Charles Galpin of Excelsior **builds first steamboat,** named the *"Governor Ramsey."* Abraham Lincoln elected president.

1862 Indian uprising at New Ulm panics local settlers; many head for safety at Fort Snelling. Others board boats to Big Island.

1867 Railroad comes to Minnetonka. First train arrives at Wayzata on the 25th of July.

1868 First propeller steamboat, the *"Sue Gardiner,"* launched by Charles Gardiner.

1869 Following the Civil War, **visitors begin arriving** from the deep south. Area seen as healthy, cool nights, and beautiful.

1879 Sir Charles Gibson opens Hotel St. Louis in Deephaven. **First major hotel** on the lake, has 200 rooms. Huge Lake Park Hotel at Tonka Bay is also completed and opened.

The Glory Years are here and Lake Minnetonka soon becomes a major resort location.

1880 Yachting is a part of "cottage life" for the well-to-do and families of businessmen who spend summers at the Lake. For others sailboats provide transportation to and from the railroad centers.

1881 1000 passenger, 160ft. **"City of St. Louis" steamboat,** owned by W. D. Washburn was launched at Wayzata on June 4th.

1882 Not to be outdone, James J. Hill builds enormous Hotel Layfayette at Minnetonka Beach, also commissions the *"Belle of Minnetonka."* The 300 foot long, 2500 passenger steamboat dwarfs all others.

A weekend cruise thru the narrows

1882 The Minnetonka Yacht Club was formed. George A. Brackett became its first Commodore. Saturday morning races during 1882, 1883 and 1884 were started off Bracketts Point, followed by lunch of bean-hole beans served by the Commodore. Beginning in 1885, the races were started in the afternoon off Lookout Point.

George Brackett

1883 A second yacht club was formed in Excelsior. Named **The Excelsior Yacht Club.**

1885 Hundreds of visitors arrive weekly. **10,000 guests were registered** in the three major hotels during June and July.
With his railroad tracks now reaching Spring Park, J.J. Hill opens Hotel Del Otero, one of the largest on the lake. It will survive for the next sixty years. **Keewaydin Hotel also opens in Cottagewood.**

1887 The *Volante* arrived from the East coast where it was built, then rigged here at Dyer's yard in Excelsior. It was a totally different design, heavy keeled, gaff-rigged, a sandbagger.

1889 The two yacht clubs merged and formed one large club. With their larger combined membership, they decided to built new docks and a clubhouse somewhere on the lake.

1890 The new clubhouse was formally opened and dedicated on July 18, 1890. The St. Louis Hotel band played to a large crowd.

1892 Heyday of the big steamboats is drawing to a close. The "Belle of Minnetonka" remains tied to the dock all summer.

1893 An incredible new sailboat, the "Onawa" was designed and built in Deephaven by Arthur Dyer for the Burton family. The *"Onawa"* sweeps every race in which it is entered.

1897 Hotel Lafayette destroyed by fire. The *Glory Years* are ending. One by one, the fabulous hotels & huge steamboats are disappearing. **Guests from the South and East are going elsewhere,** to Yellowstone, Glacier, Mackinac Island, and the East coast.

1899 Ice Boats: On September 23, the **Minnetonka Ice Club was incorporated** with Theodore Wetmore serving as its first Commodore. Within two years the club had 167 members and 17 boats. In 1904 the clubhouse caught fire and burned. It was never rebuilt.

1904 A third yacht club was formed at Excelsior as the **Minnetonka Boat Club.** A younger element in the club felt the Minnetonka Club was becoming to exclusive. Eventually differences were reconciled and in 1907 they rejoined the Minnetonka Yacht Club.

1906 A new Class A sloop, the *Wihuja,* built by Andy Peterson, owned by the Loudon brothers gained national attention for its speed and record setting times. It was known nationally as the "Minnetonka Wonder".

1911 First bridge spans the Narrows replacing a hand operated ferry, thus separating the upper and lower lake for sailboats. President Wm Howard Taft tours the lake and makes the Lafayette Club his summer White House.

1917 America prepared for war. The effect on peacetime activities like sailing was immediate. Half of the clubs young men went into the service. The Interlake races and social events were cancelled.

1943 The yacht clubhouse caught fire and was destroyed. It is a tragic loss. A committee is formed to plan a replacement building.

Yacht Club House on Light House Island

1944 It was the end of a incredible era, but the beginning of exciting new times.

(54)

Lake Minnetonka has a rich history and

YACHTING WAS AN IMPORTANT PART OF IT!

Sailboats provided needed transportation around the lake and were owned primarily by permanent summer residents. Eventually sailing and racing became so popular that it provided the lakes major social activity. This resulted in the **formation of the Minnetonka Yacht Club in 1882.** The above photo is a view from the front porch of the Hotel Del Otero which was a very large hotel located in Spring Park approximately where the Mist Condominiums are located today.

Spirit Knob in Wayzata Bay

"**Gaff-rigged**" sailboats, such as these, were popular before and around the turn of the century. In addition to the regular boom at the bottom of the sail, or foot of the sail, they had a "gaff boom" which supported the four sided sail at the top. Later sailboats utilized a Marconi rig which eliminated the gaff boom and has a triangular shaped sail that goes directly to the top of the mast. It is the principle sail type still in use today.

These boats were called *sandbaggers* as they had sand for ballast which could be moved from one side to the other as needed. They were solidly built, quite large and had enormous sails often in excess of 1000 square ft. Another popular design is known as a "catboat" and is easily recognized by the position of its mast, which is located very close to the bow. Other boats, classified as sloops, have their mast located approximately two fifths of the boat length back from the bow towards the stern.

The Glory Years of the 1880's were just getting underway when **James J. Hill,** the railroad magnate, built the massive, opulent, Hotel Lafayette at Minnetonka Beach. As part of the inaugural opening weekend on the Fourth of July, 1882, a somewhat impromptu organized sailboat race was held on the lake. **Later in the summer, the same men who had raced that day, met to form the Minnetonka Yacht Club.**

From the very beginning, the new club held regular regattas with as many as twenty boats participating. The first regatta was held August 15, 1882. George Brackett, a former Minneapolis mayor, was elected its first commodore. He was one of the lake's first sailors, and with some of his fellow residents, formed the Minnetonka Yacht Club that is now among the oldest in North America.

The clubs new flag design was a distinctive blue star on a white background with red edging.

Regatta at the Excelsior Club

A second yacht club, the Excelsior Yacht Club, was formed in 1883. Competition between the two was intense and crews were demanding a lot from their boats. Many boats were built on the East coast, some by the famous Herreshoff brothers, others by well known designers of the period. Eastern built boats, like the famous *Volante,* (still sailing on Minnetonka,) was built in a Boston yard, loaded on a railroad flat car and transported to Lake Minnetonka. **The Volante was built for Hazen Burton and his son Ward, and was the beginning of a lifetime of sailing and devotion to the Minnetonka Yacht Club.** Local boat builders, like Dyer, Moore, Brooks, Peterson and others, began turning out boats that were as good, if not better, than those coming from the East Coast, especially those built by Arthur Dyer. A series of Dyer built boats racing at both Minnetonka and on the East coast, won numerous races and championships wherever and whenever they sailed. They included: Grilse, Exit, Salmon, the incredible Onawa and many others.

The YACHT CLUB

In 1889 the two yacht clubs on the lake (the Minnetonka Yacht Club and the Excelsior Yacht Club) merged, incorporated, and formed one large club. With their larger combined membership, now totaling over 260 members, they decided to build a much needed clubhouse and new docks somewhere on the lake. Sir Charles Gibson, owner of the St. Louis Hotel, offered the yacht club a small man-made island near the entrance to Carsons Bay and $3000 dollars to get started and to help with the construction costs. **The small island known as Lighthouse Island had been created when the Bay of St. Louis had been dredged and the entrance channels widened.** An additional $3700 was pledged by others, contingent on the club raising another $2500 by March 1, 1890, and completing the clubhouse before August 1, 1890.

The first bids far exceeded the initial estimates and after submitting new plans, Harry Wild Jones was selected as the architect, with costs not to exceed $6000. Jones was a very prominent architect, having designed numerous Twin City structures including those at Lake Harriet, the Butler building, Lakewood Chapel and others.

Yacht Club Island, better known as Lighthouse Island

The dedication and formal opening was held July 18, 1890, with the band from the St. Louis Hotel playing lively music to a large crowd. Members were justly proud of their new clubhouse with its unusual architecture.

It was a very picturesque building that became a Lake Minnetonka landmark for over fifty years.

Watercolor painting of the clubhouse by artist Kurt Carlson

FAMOUS ONAWA

By 1892 racing on Lake Minnetonka had become extremely competitive with numerous Eastern built boats dominating the starting line. Boats like the Herreshoff built *Kite, Coguina* and *Alpha* were consistent winners. It seemed like they couldn't be beaten. That is, until local boat builder, Arthur Dyer, began to have great success with his latest Minnetonka boats. The *Hermes,* a Dyer catboat, won race after race throughout the 1892 season, including wins over the Herreshoff *Coquina*. Things were heating up at Minnetonka and competition was keener than ever. Hazen J. Burton, (father of Minnetonka yachting) and his son, Ward Burton, had heard that **several fast Eastern built sloops were being ordered for the 1893 Minnetonka racing season.**

At the same time, boat builder Dyer, had an idea for an entirely new concept that he felt would produce the fastest sloop ever seen at Lake Minnetonka. Mr. Burton agreed and placed an order for the first one.

This was a radically different concept, with features similar to that used in canoe design. It was to be light weight, about 200 lbs, flat-ribbed, thinly planked and canvas covered. It had no ballast, as was common for the day, instead had a thin steel center board. It was 26ft long, 6ft wide and carried only 400 sq. ft. of sail. It was designed to overhang both bow and stern, thereby riding up on top of the waves, rather than thru them.

Competing on the East Coast it won every race in which it entered and led the way to modern skow design.

ONAWA 1893

1943 Disaster: On August 31st, the clubhouse with its unique witches peaks caught fire, fanned by high winds, it was completely destroyed. Also lost were trophies, rare photographs, flags and banners. Like other Minnetonka buildings, it was a tragic loss of a historic structure and the end of a wonderful period in inland sailing history.

The cause was determined to be young boys playing with matches.

1944 Almost immediately a committee began planning construction of a new clubhouse. A corner stone was laid on August 2nd, 1944.

(56)

1896 COURSE MAP

Sandbaggers

Veruna
Wayzata Bay
1889

Hoodlum – 1910

Skow

Volante
1892

ICE BOATING

Hard Water Sailors

Ice boating got an early start on Lake Minnetonka with the formation of the *Minnetonka Ice Yacht Club* in 1899. Many of the same members that had organized the summer yacht club were also very interested in ice boating. They had been watching closely the activity on the Hudson River where ice boating was extremely popular.

Theodore Wetmore was elected the first commodore and offered his large house as a clubhouse. It was located immediately adjacent to the sailboat clubhouse at the entrance to Carsons Bay. Unfortunately it burned down a few years later in 1904. **Within the next two years the club had grown to over 160 members and had almost twenty ice boats.**

The birthplace of ice boating in America was on the Hudson River near Poughkeepsie and Hyde Park, New York. These incredible ice boats were for the most part owned by wealthy young sportsman. Almost all were built by the famous builders, Jacob and George Buckhout. Ice boating on the river ceased in 1902 when it was decided to keep the river open all winter for boat traffic. As a result, a number of their ice boats were sold to buyers living on inland lakes, including the *Northern Light* and the *Zero* which were purchased by Ward Burton and sailed on Minnetonka. Several other members purchased boats as well.

These huge boats were sometimes referred to as "Hard Water Dinosaurs" as the largest were sometimes sixty feet long and thirty feet wide, with enormous 800 square ft. sails. They could travel at outrageous speeds, covering the wide open stretches of the lower lake from Excelsior to Wayzata in a matter of minutes.

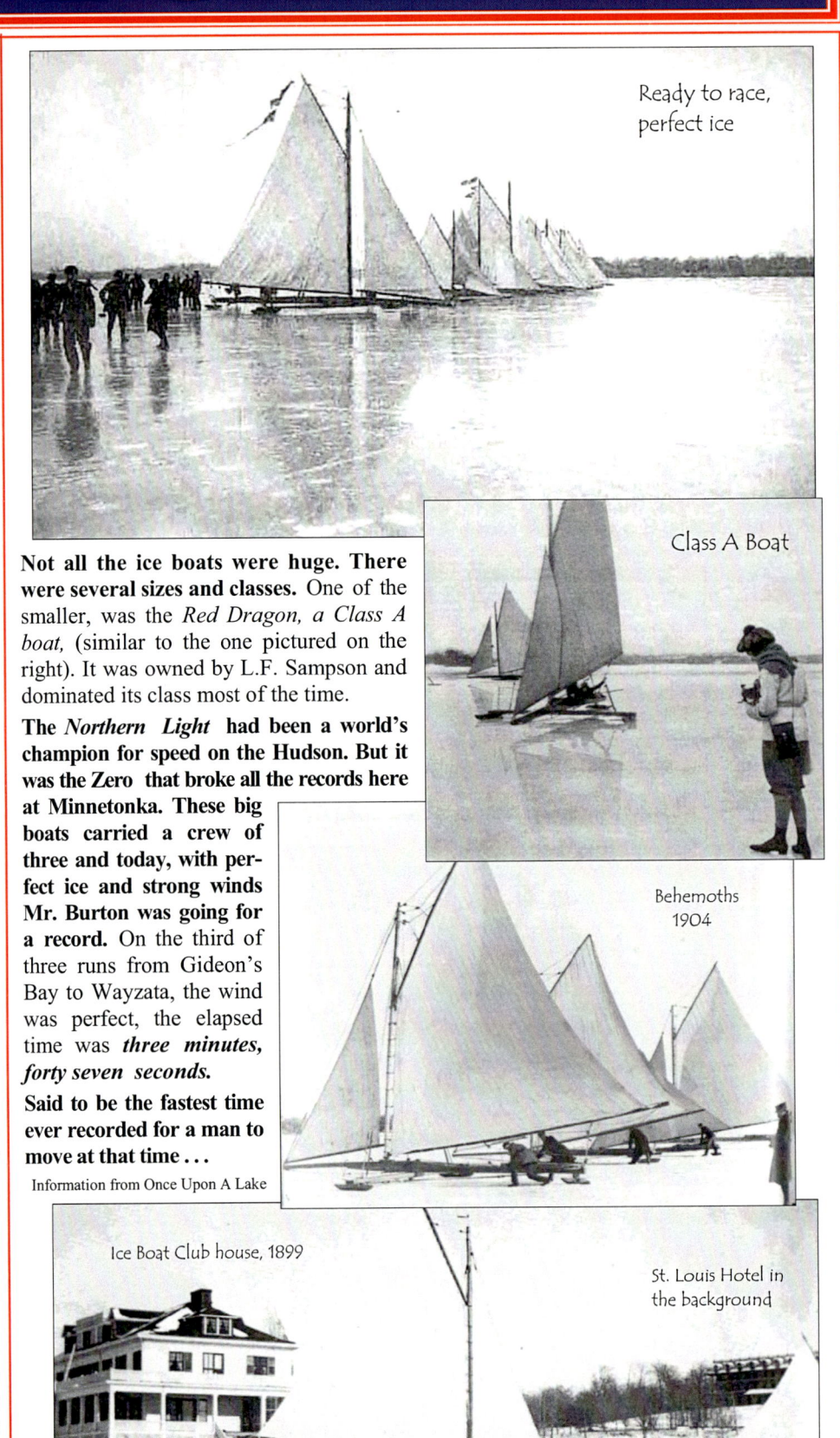

Ready to race, perfect ice

Not all the ice boats were huge. There were several sizes and classes. One of the smaller, was the *Red Dragon*, a Class A boat, (similar to the one pictured on the right). It was owned by L.F. Sampson and dominated its class most of the time.

The *Northern Light* had been a world's champion for speed on the Hudson. But it was the *Zero* that broke all the records here at Minnetonka. These big boats carried a crew of three and today, with perfect ice and strong winds Mr. Burton was going for a record. On the third of three runs from Gideon's Bay to Wayzata, the wind was perfect, the elapsed time was *three minutes, forty seven seconds.*

Said to be the fastest time ever recorded for a man to move at that time . . .

Information from Once Upon A Lake

Class A Boat

Behemoths 1904

Ice Boat Club house, 1899

St. Louis Hotel in the background

(58)

1920'S 30's & 40's

Sailing had been temporarily suspended during World War I years (1917-1919). With the war finally over and our boys returning home, sailing was slowly beginning to return. The Inland Regattas were soon revived with the Minnetonka Yacht Club hosting the races the week of August 18, 1919. Leonard Carpenter's *Helen* again won the Class C championship, as well as repeating for the 1920 Championship.

The club began its post-war season with ninety five members and a fleet of twelve A boats, four B boats, and ten C boats. Membership was not exactly booming during the 1920s—in 1923 there were only ten new members. More publicity was needed!

In an attempt to make up for not awarding trophies and silver cups during the war years, winners instead were given beautiful hand painted silk or taffeta pennants.

1932 saw the development of the X boat for younger members. Designed by the Johnson Boat Works in White Bear, it was adopted as an official class by the Inland in 1934 thus replacing the C as a starter boat.

The Interlake Regatta for 1933 was held at Minnetonka with the White Bear club victorious and claiming that Minnetonka sailors were out-sailed in every class. Minnetonka says White Bear had better boats. This was particularly true in class C where almost all the White Bear boats were Marconi rigged, and Minnetonka's boats were with the old-fashioned gaff rigs. To stay competitive Minnetonka sailors would have to upgrade.

Capsized without getting wet

Social activities were back. However, with the clubhouse located on an island and only accessible by boat, some social functions were limited. Annual banquets and other major events were often held at large local homes, area hotels or other facilities. Automobiles were rapidly changing mobility.

In 1923, the first E boat was officially adopted as an Inland Class and appeared on Lake Minnetonka in 1924.

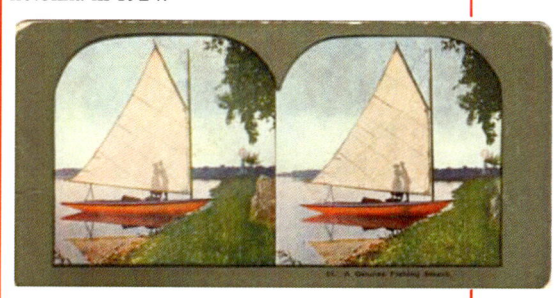

Stereo viewcards were still quite popular

Great concern in the summer of 1934 was the water level. Minnetonka was at an all time low, being about six feet below normal, the lowest in years. Diamond reef, in the middle of the bay was very close to the surface and becoming a real hazard. Many of the pilings at the club dock were entirely out of the water.

As the yacht club entered the 1940's, it had the largest fleet in its history with a total of 115 boats and a membership of 206 members.

With another World War looming on the horizon, 1941 would be the last year of the Inland Regattas, as all races would be cancelled throughout the war years. Within a few short years the majestic club house would be destroyed by a disastrous fire in 1944.

Minnetonka Yacht Clubs

With the advent of "fiberglass keel" boats in the mid 1960s, additional yacht clubs and sailing marinas appeared on the lake.

Currently operating:

The Wayzata Yacht Club: est 1965
Races keel boats. Sailing classes

Upper Minnetonka Yacht Club:
Races Saturdays, Sundays, Wed Night
Primarily keel boats

Shorewood Marina and Yacht Club
Full service sailboat marina

Sailors' World Marina & Boat Club
Sailboat dockage and sales

Minnetonka Yacht Club: est 1882
Races many classes, primarily skows

Works cited:
Virginia Brainard.Kunz, *Minnetonka Yacht Club Sailing School*. Minnetonka Yacht Club, 1982.
Blanche Nichols Wilson. *Minnetonka Story*.
The Colwell Press, Inc.1950
Thelma Jones. *Once Upon a Lake*.
Ross and Haines, Inc 1957
Miscellaneous Newspaper articles. *Northwestern Tourist,etc*
James Ogland, *Picturing Lake Minnetonka*.
Minnesota Historical Society 2001
Ellen Wilson Myer. *Tales of Tonka* 1993
Excelsior Lake Minnetonka Historical Society Publications

SAILING CLOSE

Mound

Great Fishing

Lake Minnetonka

A HISTORICAL INSIGHT

MOUND

By Jim Ogland, author of
"Picturing Lake Minnetonka"

©DNALGO Enterprises Box 935 Wayzata, Mn 55391

Harrison's Bay, Lake Minnetonka

MOUND.... TIME LINE

1851 Important "Traverse de Sioux and Mendota Treaties" **are signed with Indians,** opening way for pioneer settlement.

1852 Simon Stevens and Calvin Tuttle *rediscover* Lake Minnetonka, **build a dam and sawmill** at Minnetonka Mills.

1853 First hotel in lake area opens, located at Minnetonka Mills. Governor Alexander Ramsey visits lake. After learning that Indians call it "Min-ni-tanka," he officially names it Minnetonka.

1854 The "Pre-emption Privilege Act" is extended to Minnesota Territory. Allows settlers to stake a claim. Mathias S. Cook is the first settler to arrive in Mound. **Cook House built in Mound.** Cook's hotel is later named the Lake View House.

1855 Frank Halstead arrives and purchases thirty acres on Halsteds Bay. Builds a log cabin on a small clearing. Other settlers from the East also arriving.

1858 Minnesota admitted to the Union. **Becomes the 32nd state** on May 11, 1858.

1860 Rev. Charles Galpin of Excelsior **builds first steamboat,** named the *"Governor Ramsey."* Lincoln elected president.

1861 Civil War begins. Minnesotans and others join the ranks. Conflict lasts four years until 1865.

1862 Indian uprising at New Ulm panics local settlers, many head for safety at Fort Snelling. Others board boats to Big Island.

1867 Railroad comes to Minnetonka. First train arrives at Wayzata on the 25th of July opening a new era of transportation.

1868 Captain Frank Halstead returns from Civil War and builds new cabin named the "Hermitage." He becomes the first Hermit of Lake Minnetonka, a tourist attraction.

1869 Following the Civil War, vistors arrive from the deep South. Area seen as healthy, cool nights, and beautiful. Frank and Benton Carmen start a freight boat business between Mound and Wayzata.

1870 New, wider, deeper channel is dredged at the Narrows thus allowing larger steamboats to come to Mound from Excelsior, Wayzata and the Lower Lake.

1875 General Store opens in Mound by Hill Griggs to serve cordwood business woodcutters. **Frank Halstead builds a large steamboat** named the *"Mary."* **Chapman House is built on lakeshore and opens July 4, 1876.**

1876 Mound City is recognized. The small settlement at the intersection of Bartlett and Commerce Boulevards is named for numerous Indian burial mounds in the area. A significant number of developments take place in 1876. A post office and sawmill are established. During the summer, the Lake View House had 1000 registered guests; the Chapman House had 700. Two steamers, the *May Queen* and the *Mary* brought tourists to Mound. **General George Armstrong Custer is killed at the battle of the Little Big Horn.**

1879 Sir Charles Gibson opens Hotel St. Louis in Deephaven. **First major hotel** on the lake, 200 rooms. Huge Lake Park Hotel at Tonka Bay is also completed and open.

1882 James J. Hill builds enormous Hotel Layfayette at Mtka. Beach. Also commissions *"Belle of Minnetonka."* **The 300 foot steamboat dwarfs all others.**

1883 Ed Bartlett builds Bartlett Place Hotel next to the Lost Lake channel. The Mound City House is built in 1884 and operated by John Chapman. *Glory Years* **at Minnetonka are here. Hundreds of visitors arrive weekly. 10,000 guests were registered in the lakes three major hotels during June & July.**

1885 With his railroad tracks now reaching Spring Park, J.J. Hill opens the Hotel Del Otero. One of the largest on the lake. It will survive for the next sixty years. Tourism is Mound City's life blood. It provides new businesses and jobs for domestics, and others. Restaurants are full, hotels are overflowing. Times are good, these are peak tourist years at Lake Minnetonka. Residents and resort owners are prospering.

1892 Heyday of the big steamboats is drawing to a close. *"Belle of Minnetonka"* remains tied to the dock all summer.

1897 Hotel Lafayette destroyed by fire. The *Glory Years* are ending. One by one, the fabulous hotels & huge steamboats are disappearing. **Guests from the South and East are going elsewhere.**

1899 New hotels being built, the **Dewey house** in 1899 and the **Buena Vista Hotel** in 1902. The Upper Lake is noted for good fishing.

1900 With the arrival of the railroad, the city center shifts from the lakeshore to the depot location. In 1906, a canal is dredged in an effort to bring the lake to the new uptown business district. During summer months fifteen to sixteen hundred tourists arrive daily. Trains connect six times a day with specials on Sundays. **The Baptist Bible Church Camp Assembly Grounds** in the Highlands is a very popular spot for young and old. Numerous cottages and tents dot the grounds. A Casino is built on the lakeshore by Mrs. John Chapman for her son, Cecil. **Later becomes the popular Surfside.**

1905 *Golden Years arrive.* **Excelsior residents awake to the rumble of streetcars on Water Street.** Thomas Lowry's Twin City Rapid Transit Company is about to forever change Lake Minnetonka.

1910 Neighboring communities of Three Points and Island Park are developing as summer cottage locations. Local neighborhood grocery stores have sprung up to serve their needs at: Avalon, Wychwood, Pembrook, Chester Park, Three Points, etc.

1912 Mound incorporated as a village. Elections are held for the first time. The area of the new village was eleven hundred acres. Population was 276. The automobile is arriving, transportation becomes easier. Cottages are springing up.

1917 A new three story consolidated school was built and served the district until 1963 when it caught fire and burned. Roaring Twenties are just around the corner: prohibition, Charleston, raccoon coats.

Early Settlement

For hundreds of years, **Lake Minnetonka** and the land surrounding it had belonged to the Dakota-Sioux Indians and other tribes. It was one of their most favored places in the entire northwest. This was about to change as negotiations were in progress to acquire a large section of the remaining un-ceded lands in the new Minnesota Territory. The acquisition by treaty-purchase included much of the land west of the Mississippi (southern and western Minnesota), **and the land surrounding Mound and Lake Minnetonka.** The treaties of Traverse des Sioux and Mendota were officially signed on July 23 and August 5, 1851. Indian title or rights of occupancy to Lake Minnetonka, however, were not fully extinguished until: A) The treaties were amended and ratified by the U.S. Senate (which occurred in 1852) B) The amendments accepted by the Sioux and C) The treaties proclaimed by President Fillmore on Feb. 24, 1853.

The signing of the important 1851 Traverse des Sioux treaty

The following September, the resident Indian bands finally departed the area for agencies established in the open prairie on the upper Mississippi. U.S. policy during this period did not legally permit any settlement on non-government owned lands; furthermore, the newly acquired lands had to be properly surveyed before they would be offered for sale to would-be landowners and settlers. The surveys were begun in early 1853, with township lines being surveyed first in the fall of 1854, and subdivision lines the spring of 1855.

The Homestead Act was still a dream, but with the act of August 4, 1854, the *"preemption privilege"* was finally extended to settlers on the un-surveyed lands of Minnesota territory. The first settlers, however, had not waited for the *"preemption privilege"* or for the surveys to be completed or even started, but began staking out "claims" immediately after receiving word that the treaties had been signed. They invaded the un-surveyed land and began cutting timber, building mills and opening roads. These settlers became known as "squatters," and by staking out the boundaries of their claim and protecting it by building a claim shack or shanty, they could later, when the surveys were completed, file their claim and purchase the land. They could purchase up to 160 acres at $125.00 an acre and receive a deed that made them "original landowners."

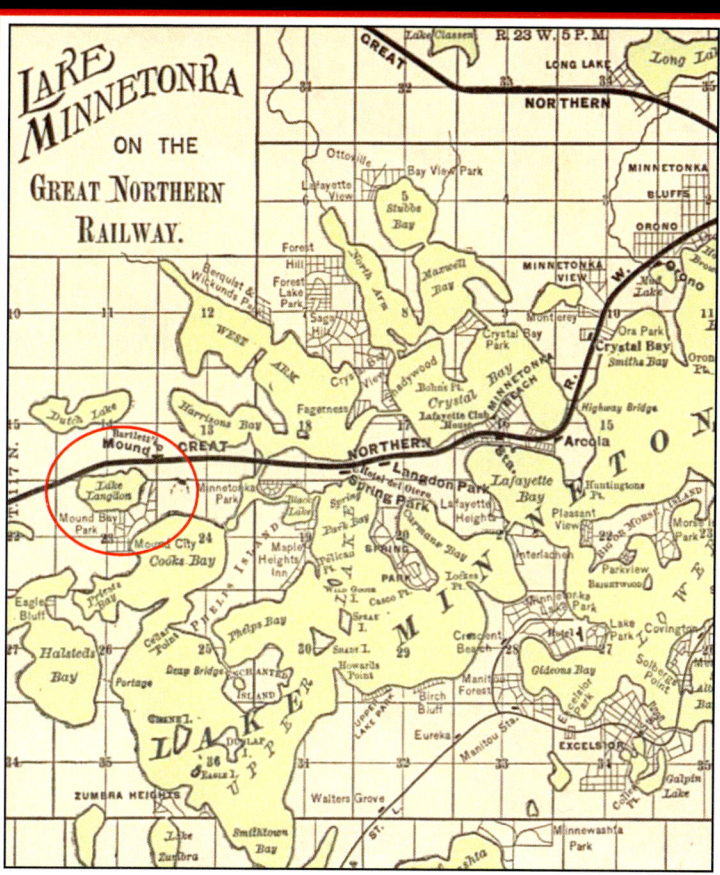

Map of the western half of Lake Minnetonka, shows Mound City

The far western shoreline was one of the last areas to be settled. **Among the first to arrive in 1854, and stake a claim, was Mathias S. Cook. He was the first settler and built the first log cabin in what is now the city of Mound.** His father-in-law, John Carman, with his family from Ohio, were among the earliest arrivals at Lake Minnetonka, he staked out an early claim on Carmans Bay in 1853. Mathias Cook had married Miss Anna Carman in 1850 and it was her father who had encouraged the couple to join them and settle in Minnesota. Carman's sons, Frank and Benton, later operated a freight boat business between Mound and Wayzata. The Cook's log cabin served as a stop-over place in Mound for numerous travelers and settlers who passed through the area, **eventually it became known as Cooks' Hotel and was later enlarged and re-named the Lake View House.**

Lake View House

A second early settler was Captain Frank Halstead who arrived at the lake in 1855, and purchased thirty acres of land on what is now known as Halsteads Bay (on some maps spelled Halsteds). He was a colorful character with a long history and became very well known around the lake.

As more and more pioneers began arriving, the beginning of a new community started to develop, Mound City. The center of which was located on the lake at the intersection of rudimentary roads known today as Commerce Boulevard and Bartlett Boulevard.

Lodging / Tourists

After Hennepin County had been established in 1858, the county commissioners set aside the southwestern corner as (Township No.117 N. Range 24 W.) and named it Minnetrista Township. Each township was 36 square miles. Mound City fell within these boundaries and was governed by the township board of supervisors until 1912, when Mound City separated by incorporating as the Village of Mound. There was a constable and a justice of the peace that kept law and order. The territorial census of 1860 showed fifty two families with a population of two hundred and thirteen now residing within Minnetrista township.

Mound was growing, but the Civil War was about to begin (1861) and many young men would be asked to volunteer for service in the Union Army.

The first post office was established in 1856 and the first log school houses were built in 1861. A much needed blacksmith shop was established in 1866. Major development of the new village would soon come in the 1870's.

After serving during the Civil War in the Union Navy, Captain Frank Halstead returned to his property on Cook's Bay. Now known as the "Hermitage" his cabin was enlarged and became a point of interest and curiosity for visitors to the area. He built the 78 ft steamboat, *"Mary,"* which for many years became an active passenger steamboat on the Upper Lake.

His untimely drowning death the day before the *Mary* was to be launched was ruled a suicide.

The Captain's brother, George, also a Navy man came to settle his affairs and ended up staying the rest of his life.

The "Hermitage" on Cook's Bay
(Was located on County Road 44)

George was well educated and a gentleman, but like his brother, lived alone and was also considered a hermit. He took over, launched and operated the steamboat "Mary," successfully for a number of years.

Shortly after the end of the Civil War, Lake Minnetonka began to be recognized as an ideal location to visit and vacation. The weather was cool, refreshing and healthful. Arriving guests needed lodging and dining.

MINNESOTA'S FAMOUS RESORT NEAR THE TWIN CITIES

In 1875, the Chapman brothers built a three story hotel on the waterfront. The following spring of 1876 they expanded with a three story addition that now had thirty five rooms. The new hotel opened with a bang on the fourth of July, 1876.

The Chapman House on Cook's Bay

A typical family summer resort with good food and great fishing, it soon became one of the most popular hotels on the Upper Lake. It had a wonderful bathing beach and docking for numerous boats. In 1906, a large pavilion was built on the property just steps away from the waterfront. It became known as the *Mound Casino* and in later years, as the Surfside. The second level was a huge roller skating rink which was used for dances and wedding receptions. It remained a popular restaurant and night spot into the 1980's.

In 1870, the Narrows Channel separating the Upper from the Lower Lake, was widened and re-dredged, thus allowing large steamboats to travel to Mound and the Upper Lake.

Mathias Cook, pioneer hotel keeper of the Upper Lake, already had some lodging available at his Cook's House, but more would soon be needed. In addition to vacationers, a cordwood business was being started in the area. Wood cutters with the Northwestern Fuel and Lumber Company were operating in the nearby woods and needed lodging. In 1875, Hill Griggs and Company of St. Paul, established a general store in Mound to serve the woodcutters needs.

LAKE VIEW HOTEL 1876

In 1876, Mathias Cook replaced his earlier log hotel with a new three story structure which greatly improved its capacity and amenities. It now had both suites and rooms with good views of the lake. During the 1876 summer, the hotel registered over 1000 guests. It also featured facilities for invalids, as the lake was becoming well known for its healthful location.

Mound had a surprising number of moderately priced family hotels.

Among them were the **Dewey House,** located eastward along the shore and was a quiet and healthful place with low rates. The **Mound City Hotel** was a smaller comfortable hotel that opened in 1884. Another well known hotel was the **Palmer House,** located at Zumbra Heights. It was billed as a health resort.

BARTLETT PLACE HOTEL
Cottages and Boat House

"To those contemplating a trip to this most beautiful lake, for rest, solid comfort, good fishing and pleasure without being compelled to be in full dress at all hours, this place will be your ideal. Bait and oarsman are always at hand."

THE BUENA VISTA HOTEL

Located westward from Chapman's in the Mound Highlands, it was a relative latecomer to Lake Minnetonka. It was never-the-less a very popular summer hotel catering to vacationers who wanted a quiet restful time. Like many hotels, its appearance changed over the years.

Steamers / Tours / Islands

Lake Minnetonka — You Must See It

Finally, in 1900, the Great Northern Railroad extended its passenger and freight line from Spring Park to Mound, thus bringing tourists and visitors directly from Minneapolis and St. Paul to the developing village of Mound and the lake. Whether coming to the lake for a day or a week, this provided a much needed connection to the expanding tourist interest in the Upper Lake.

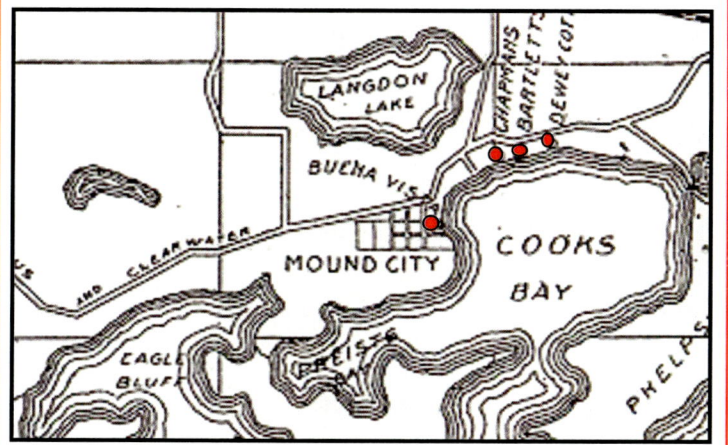

Location of Chapmans, Bartletts, Dewey and Buena Vista Hotels

Generally speaking, Lake Minnetonka is 20 miles long and 4 miles wide, with a charmingly irregular shore line of over 100 miles. Its channels, islands, and bays are continually revealing new vistas of dancing waters, and its shores are dotted with handsome summer homes, hotels and club houses. The lake is alive with sailboats, launches, motorboats and steamboats, all adding life and color to the beautiful scene.

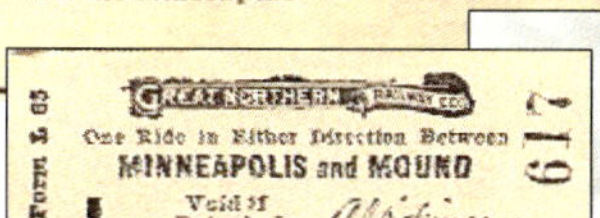

The 1880's & 1890's had established Lake Minnetonka as a major tourist destination, but now the same railroads that had been bringing tourists here were taking them elsewhere. No longer were the wealthy southerners and affluent easterners coming to Minnetonka. Early 1900's tourists were now mainly from Minnesota and nearby states. An important visitors' area during this period was the **"Baptist Church Assembly Grounds,"** located in the Highlands of Mound, just west of Chapmans. In the summer months, six scheduled trains a day brought as many as sixteen hundred tourists to Mound. Many walked the short distance to the lakefront hotels, cottages or the assembly grounds; others rode in livery wagons or carriages. These summer guests were occupied with numerous water activities including: swimming, rowing, fishing and sailing was also popular. Many attending the Assembly Grounds sessions slept in tents and ate at the large dining hall.

By the turn of the century the tourist trade was still strong, but changing. Many tourists no longer arrived by steamboat as they had in the past. The railroads were now the major way of transportation to the lake. **The new Narrows channel and the bridge at the Seton channel greatly improved access to Mound.** The roads leading to Mound were at best rough and the new fangled automobiles were often mired down. Still Henry Ford's Model T was taking over from the horse drawn liveries and carriages. Hotels, cottages and boarding houses were in high demand and were often filled to capacity. The locals prospered along with the hotels as jobs of all descriptions were needed. Boat fleets needed operators, fishing guides were in demand, domestics and food service helpers of all kinds were required. **During the "Glory Years," (the eighties and nineties) steamboat tours of the Upper Lake were very popular and numerous steamers and larger steamboats provided daily scheduled tours into the Upper Lake.** The two largest and best known steamboats were the *City of St. Louis* and the *Belle of Minnetonka.* They were huge and could accommodate hundreds of passengers. Each day they met the early train in Wayzata, and with whistles blowing, raced each other to Excelsior. (Then on thru the narrows into the Upper Lake, past the numerous islands and land marks and on to Mound.) The *Mary* and the *May Queen* were smaller, but very popular Upper Lake steamers that provided three hour tours of the lake and its many islands. The *May Queen* could handle 75 passengers and the 78 ft *Mary* could carry 100. Visitors were always curious about the "Hermitage" and sometimes the boats would stop for a visit. There was great interest in the numerous Indian burial mounds that had been discovered in the area. **A cluster of small islands are located between Cook's Bay and Smithtown Bay. Some had summer cabins on them. The islands were all privately owned and had been sub-divided into lots and available as building sites. Crane Island became the most developed and had numerous cabins. Wawatasso, also called Boy Scout Island, was used as a scout camp for many years. Eagle Island was never developed and has remained wild and natural. These islands along with Goose Island and Spray Island in Spring Park Bay were only accessible by boat. Three much larger, nearby islands connected to Mound by bridges are: Phelps, Enchanted, and Shady Island. Phelps Island, also known as Island Park, was later annexed by Mound in 1960.**

The Puritan

The May Queen

The Plymouth

Shady Island, initially only accessible by boat, had a large hotel (Harrow House) operated by Major Thomas Harrow. The island property owners had a unique association much like todays condo associations. There was also a University students camp.

Shady Island, Harrow House

With the coming of the railroad, the city center and business district of Mound was shifting from the lakeshore near Chapmans, to uptown around the new train station. This was a concern of the hotel and lakeshore owners as they wanted a connection with the depot and the new post office. The digging of a canal across Lost Lake was suggested and a 30ft wide canal was approved and work began. Initially, the canal provided the needed connection, but soon proved unsuccessful as the marsh land began to fill back in with mud, etc.

Upper Lake

Lake Minnetonka is not just one large body of water, but rather a number of smaller lakes all connected together by channels. **There are four types of lakes in the world and Minnetonka is three of them.** The lake was created by two different glaciers over 10,000 years apart. One glacier created the Lower Lake on one side of the Narrows and another glacier the Upper Lake on the other side of the Narrows Channel. Because of the trace minerals and other factors left behind by the receding glaciers, the aquatic life, vegetation and chemistry is different in the Upper and Lower Lakes. Thus the fish are different in various parts of the lake. The Lower Lake resembles Northern Minnesota lakes, whereas the Upper Lake more closely resembles the prairie lakes of southwestern Minnesota.

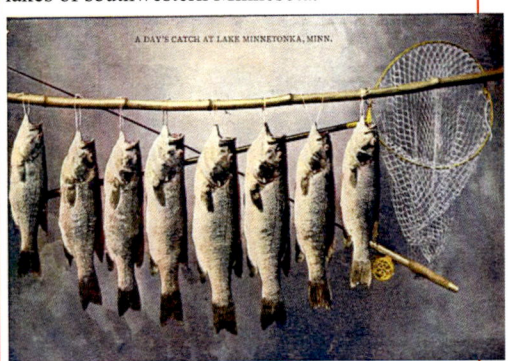

Fishing was important

It has been reported that the largest concentration of game fish is to be found in the Upper Lake and Northern Bays. **Chapman's resort in Mound always advertised that more fish were to be found in the Upper Lake because it was fished less.** Minnetonka includes many varieties of fish such as: sunfish, crappies, perch, northern pike, walleyes, pickerel, black crappies, small mouth bass, rock bass, and black bass. Many tourists came to the lake just to fish. Their visits continued to help support the local economy.

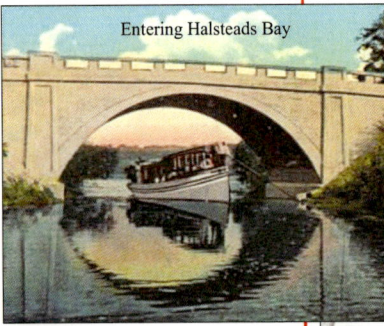

Halstead's Bay is the most western bay and one of the shallowest. It has good cover and good habitat which is always important to good fishing. The best perch beds are reportedly located in Halstead's Bay. Also nice size blue gills and pumpkinseeds can be found here and throughout the lake.

This was the lakeshore boathouse and fishing rowboat rental dock at Chapmans. It was one of four locations on Cook's Bay that had bait, tackle and rental boats. Guides were also available.

MOUND was the largest and the major town on the Upper Lake.
By the turn-of-the-century Mound residents were experiencing a different life style than their rural Minnetrista Township neighbors. Theirs was more agricultural while Mound was urban and livelihoods were often connected directly with the lake. Many residents felt that incorporation as a village would be beneficial, however, enough favorable votes to incorporate was not achieved until an election that was held in January of 1912.
1902 saw a number of service improvements: Rural mail delivery was implemented and residents no longer were required to pick up their own mail. The very first telephone service to Mound was started with the installation of three telephones.
For years Mound was the center of most activity at this end of the lake. The Mound "Pilot" was the weekly newspaper and printed the latest news. Three doctors practiced in Mound. The Mound State Bank was here, as was the area Post Office, the hardware store, several restaurants and the Mound Senior High School. Over the years there were a number of different school buildings, many of which caught fire and were destroyed.

Stringers like this one of northern pike and bass were common

This postcard photo is near Pelican Point on Island Park in Spring Park Bay. The location was close to Woolnoughs Hotel, also known as Maple Heights, then later as Tipiwaukon. The boat was probably from there or rented from the nearby Hotel Del Otero. Adjacent Goose Island was a known area for good bass fishing.

Postcards such as this camping scene were available and hundreds of Minnetonka cards were purchased and mailed. Tent camping was enjoyed throughout the lake area as it was inexpensive and fun. A popular remote spot was Hardscrabble Point located in Priests Bay. Big Island owner, W.B. Morse, sold lots on the island and had tents and camping equipment for rent.

The first Minnetonka Yacht Club was formed in 1881 with a fleet of twenty boats and is still active today. These gaff rigged sandbaggers pictured here on the Upper Lake in front of the Hotel del Otero carried 800 square feet of sail and over 800 lbs of ballast. Many great sailing regattas have been hosted on the lake.

The Roaring Twenties

The automobile had arrived! In the 1920's ordinary people became less dependent on public transportation. With the coming of the automobile came the construction of better roads. People traveled faster and further and soon discovered that Lake Minnetonka was not so far. Cottages were springing up in Mound and around the lake.

Despite the fascination with the new automobiles, and the mobility that they provided, hundreds of visitors still came every weekend to Lake Minnetonka. They came to fish or to just enjoy being near the water. During the week the growing resident population rode the fast express boats to the train stations and to work in the Twin Cities. As the years went by, the lake continued to attract more and more residents. Summer cottages became year around homes and the larger towns, Excelsior, Wayzata and Mound built new schools and churches to accommodate the increasing population. **Like each preceding decade, the roaring twenties brought new changes to Lake Minnetonka.** Chief among them was the drawing to a close of the streetcar/steamboat era.

A day trip to Lake Minnetonka

HIAWATHA

Mound

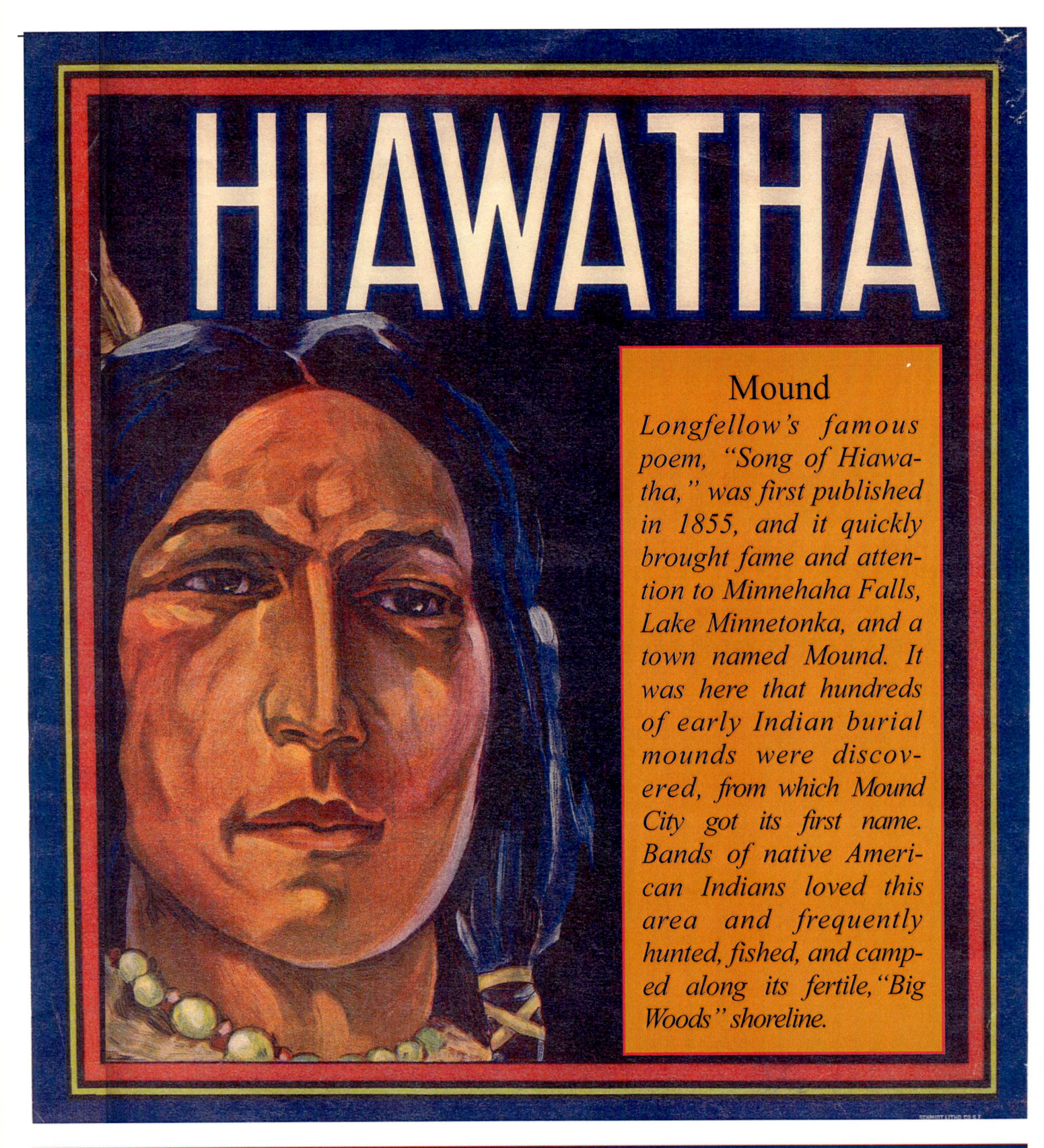

Longfellow's famous poem, "Song of Hiawatha," was first published in 1855, and it quickly brought fame and attention to Minnehaha Falls, Lake Minnetonka, and a town named Mound. It was here that hundreds of early Indian burial mounds were discovered, from which Mound City got its first name. Bands of native American Indians loved this area and frequently hunted, fished, and camped along its fertile, "Big Woods" shoreline.

Mighty Dakota Indians camped around Cooks

A new kind of tourist was coming

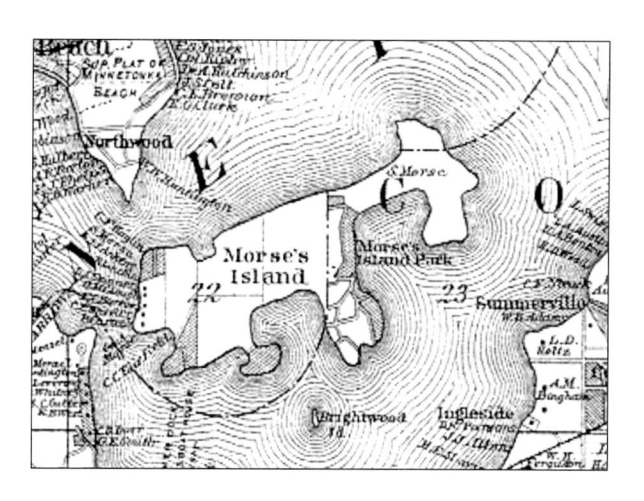

A tourist just for the day

Lake Minnetonka

A HISTORICAL INSIGHT

LAKE MINNETONKA TOWER POSTCARD, BIG ISLAND PARK 1906

BIG ISLAND

EARLY HISTORY: 1850'S, TURN OF THE CENTURY & BIG ISLAND AMUSEMENT PARK

By Jim Ogland, author of "Picturing Lake Minnetonka"

DNALGO Enterprises Box 935 Wayzata, Mn 55391

BIG ISLAND - A HISTORIC INSIGHT
A chronological record of Big Island's early history

Big Island's history began thousands of years ago in the Ice Age when the great glaciers carved out the area and the Lake Minnetonka, basin. Long before the early explorers discovered it, the waters of Minnetonka with its many bays and peninsulas, was a sacred place and a favorite hunting ground of early Indian inhabitants. Many a battle was fought between the Dakota-Sioux and the Chippewa or Ojibway, for its coveted bays and headlands. **French trappers referred to Minnetonka as *"lac gros"* in the *"grand bois,"* "Big Lake in the Woods."**

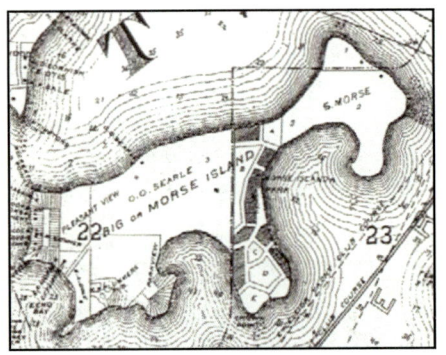

1800's Principal inhabitants of Lake Minnetonka were the "Mighty Dahkotah." They came often to Minnetonka for ceremonies and celebrations. Over four hundred Indian burial mounds were discovered around the lake. Big Island is situated in the middle of the lower lake and contains about 275 acres. It is actually made up of three separate islands. Two large areas are divided by a north-south channel, and a smaller third area is named Mahpiyata Island.

1822 First discovery by white men came in May of 1822, when two young boys, one a drummer boy from nearby Fort Snelling, paddled their canoe up Minnehaha Creek. **They explored the lake and camped overnight on Big Island.** Their discovery, however, went unnoticed for an additional thirty years.

1851 Important "Traverse des Sioux and Mendota Treaties" were **signed with Indians,** opening way for pioneer settlement.

Chief Little Crow: Spokesman for the Sioux and first Indian signer of the Traverse des Sioux and Mendota Treaties

1852 Early settlers, Simon Stevens and Calvin Tuttle, re-discovered Lake Minnetonka, built a dam and sawmill at Minnetonka Mills. Governor Alexander Ramsey visits lake. After learning that Indians call it "Min-ni (water) tan-ka (big), he officially names it Minnetonka.

Big Island becomes first known as Owens Island for a Colonel John P. Owens who had accompanied Governor Ramsey. Then became known as Meekers Island, after Judge Bradley B. Meeker, who had staked an early claim to the island. Prior to this, the island was known as Cottage Island, presumably because of the Indian cottages built there, not the usual tepees made of lodge poles and covered with hides, but shelters or cottages built of timbers.

The Indians themselves referred to the Island as "Wetutanka." The Dakota word "Wetu" means *"the springtime move to sugaring camp,"* and "tanka" means "great." An appropriate name as the island was the Indian's main sugar camp, where they annually tapped the giant sugar maples and boiled the sap for maple sugar.

> **Many myths and legends, both historical and mythical are centered around Big Island.** Perhaps the best known is the Legend of Mahpiyata, *"celestial peace maiden"* daughter of Chief Wakanyeya. A daring party of young Ojibway warriors came down from the north to raid the favorite Minnetonka hunting and fishing ground of their hereditary enemy and to win their coveted eagle plumes by taking back a prized scalp-lock or two of the "Mighty Dahcotah," as well as game and fish. During the ensuing battle, the handsome Ojibway leader captured the beautiful Mahpiyata and claimed her for his own wigwam, and took her back to the north where they eventually married. After numerous years of warfare there was peace between the tribes and at the length of many winters, they returned to Big Island and were laid to rest side by side on the northerly end of the island. So ends the legend.
> (Abridged)

1856 The island was acquired by W.B. Morse and his brother, John. They developed, platted and sold lots for cottages. **It became known as Morse or Big Island and eventually after 1906 with the opening of the Big Island Amusement Park simply as Big Island.**

1858 Minnesota admitted to the Union, and becomes the 32th state on May 11, 1858.

1862 Indian uprising at New Ulm panics local settlers; many head for safety at Fort Snelling. **Others board boats to Big Island.**

1867 Railroad comes to Minnetonka. First train arrives at Wayzata on the 25th of July.

1869 Following the Civil War, **many visitors begin arriving** from the deep south. Area is seen as healthy, and beautiful with cool nights.

1880's W.B. Morse by this time had sold most of his lots and a number of families have built cottages on the island. Tenting is very popular and Morse leases tents to overnight campers.

1891 Olaf O. Searles, a wealthy Minneapolis banker and entrepreneur, bought almost half of the Island (125 acres) on which he built a magnificent three story, 21 room mansion, with steam heat and gas lights. He also created a beautifully landscaped formal estate and hired immigrant labor to dig a channel across the Island which then separated his property from neighbors towards the west. This also created a sizable lagoon and the triangular shaped Mahpiyata Island.

Bridge connecting Mahpiyata Island

1892 Heyday of the big steamboats is drawing to a close. *"Belle of Minnetonka"* remains tied to the dock all summer.

1900 By the end of the century, the wealthy tourists, who had helped turn Lake Minnetonka into one of the regions premier resort destinations, were vacationing elsewhere. It appeared that Lake Minnetonka was on its way to becoming just another affluent suburb. **Minnetonka was sleeping, but not for long!**

1905 Excelsior residents awoke early one morning to the rumble of streetcars. **A new kind of tourist was coming to the lake.** They were coming just for the day, **they were excited,** they were looking for summer fun. It was the dawn of a new era.

1906 Thomas Lowry and his Twin City Rapid Transit company were about to change Lake Minnetonka and Big Island forever. He envisioned Minnetonka as a vast recreational location for thousands of visitors from nearby Minneapolis and St. Paul.

A new kind of tourist !

The Glory Years at Lake Minnetonka were gone ! The wealthy southerners are vacationing elsewhere. In their place are local excursionists and *a new kind of tourist, a tourist that would come to the lake just for the day.* There was a new freedom in the air, a new mood, a new century! People needed and wanted mobility. They wanted recreation and good times. They wanted to escape from their everyday lives, if only for the weekend.

BIG ISLAND PICNIC AND AMUSEMENT PARK . . . 1906-1911

The lights on the Big Island Tower could be seen from all points on the lake. It was an impressive and spectacular sight! In 1905 the Twin City Rapid Transit Company (TCRT) created the Lake Minnetonka Division. They would extend their streetcar line from Minneapolis to Excelsior, then to Deephaven and eventually to Tonka Bay. **Next they would build a large (65 acre) picnic and amusement park on Big Island in the center of Lake Minnetonka** and acquire the huge Tonka Bay Hotel. They would assemble a fleet of unique steamboats to provide "on time" scheduled transportation to all points on the lake. Six fast seventy foot Express Boats were built specifically to radiate out from the Excelsior docks on four separate routes to twenty seven ports of call. *A wonderful exciting time, and a new era was unfolding for Lake Minnetonka.*

Getting to the lake and Big Island was half the fun!

Riding the fast, yellow interurban streetcars, *which often reached speeds of 60 miles per hour, was alone worth the trip.* It was daring, sometimes breathtaking, thrilling, and very exciting!

The return trip after dark was even more spectacular as the streetcars seemed to fly back to the cities on the brilliantly lit line. The route was labeled the "Great White Way."

Streetcars brought passengers from both Minneapolis and St. Paul to Excelsior where **they were unloaded at the dock station** for the two mile trip to Big Island Park.

The Big Island Ferryboats: Anticipating the need for large crowds to be transported from Excelsior to Big Island, the Twin City Rapid Transit Company built three large double ended ferryboats. Each had a capacity of 1000 passengers. They were 142 feet in length, 39 feet wide and had three passenger decks. With a steering wheel and a rudder on either end, the need to turn around was eliminated. **These boats were designated for large capacity shuttle service between the Excelsior Dock Station and the Big Island Amusement Park.** They were powered by steam boilers which in turn were fired by soft coal. They were surprisingly fast and made the round trip to Big Island in approximately fifty minutes. On weekends and holidays one departed from Excelsior every twenty minutes. They made the park easy to get to, and for many, a chance to be on the water. Sometimes as many as 15,000 people a day visited the park. **They were named** the *Minneapolis,* the *Minnetonka* and the *St. Paul.* Final versions of the ferryboats were painted white to set them apart from the others.

1000 passenger ferryboat, Minneapolis

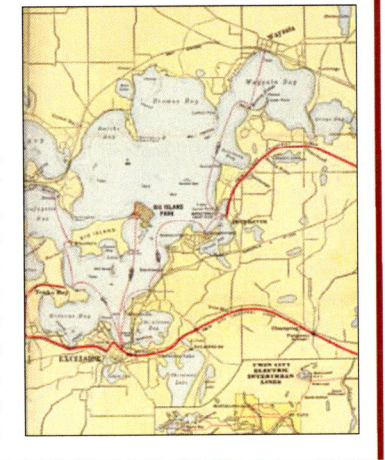

Steamboats of all types and sizes were continuously arriving at the docks. In addition to the large ferrys, the company owned and operated excursion boats. They were the *Excelsior, Plymouth* and the *Puritan.* These three boats made daily three hour panoramic tours of the lake. The round trip fare was 25 cents. A fourth boat, the smaller capacity *Mayflower,* was used for special occasions. All boats, however, were open to charters, sightseeing, or special excursion parties for either day or night trips. Tours of both the lower, as well as the upper lake and islands, were available. Other TCRT boats included the six yellow streetcar boats. They were built primarily for and designated to run specific routes to all points on the lake. However, they occasionally stopped at Big Island Park with concert passengers or special runs.

Excursion boats Excelsior, Victor and Puritan at Tonka Bay

BIG ISLAND PARK OPENS

In March, 1906, the Twin City Rapid Transit Company sponsored a contest to name the new park it was building. Hundreds of people around the country sent in suggestions. In the end TCRT chose "Big Island Park." The park opened informally on April 27th with service provided by one ferryboat and two express boats. Construction of the park continued through the spring and into the summer. Finally, on August 5, 1906, the park officially opened - unfinished, but with plenty to see and do. Among the amusements that first day were a roller coaster and an "old mill" boat ride thru a dark tunnel. *(This ride is still operating at the State Fair each year.)* While it was essentially a picnic resort, several inexpensive and attractive amusement features added to the Island's activities.

Above is an artist's aerial view of the park. The park, which included many unique features, was designed by noted architect, *Leroy Buffington.* He also designed the Tonka Bay Hotel and numerous other Lake Minnetonka structures.

Great Outings

Big Island soon became the destination point for many weekend fun-seekers. Church groups and fraternal organizations were scheduling their picnics and outings on the island. Individuals, families and many small groups also came. On arrival, there was lots of exploring to do. Paths were laid out along the "Peristyles" (arched concrete walls that followed the ridges). Despite the heat of the day, the island paths always seemed cool and inviting. The grass was neatly trimmed and everything was well cared for. **Steamboats were coming and going.** They sounded their magnificent steam whistles as they departed from the island. **Big Island Park was a large operation** and required considerable behind the scenes support activity. There was an ice house, a stable for the work horses, separate dormitories for men and women, a maintenance shop, a mess hall for island employees. The sixty five acres required daily maintenance which in turn provided numerous jobs for local residents. Hotels and rooming houses benefited as well.

By streetcar, by train, by boat they came!

These two Mission style structures adorned either side of the steps leading from the dock area to the "Main Walkway" and the 200 ft Light Tower. They anchored the main "Peristyle" (arched walls) that followed the high ground and ridges over much of the island. Shown here, in about 1915 in disrepair, with the park now closed and nearly abandoned. *(Foundations and steps still exist today.)* One of the only reminders of what was once here over 100 years ago.

The Twin City Rapid Transit Company had gained considerable experience from their similar amusement park operation at Wildwood. *Wildwood Amusement Park* was located at White Bear Lake, just north of St. Paul. With a destination location on either side of the Twin Cities, the Company hoped to attract residents and visitors alike to ride their streetcars and visit Lake Minnetonka.

The landing showing the construction scaffolding in the background surrounding the uncompleted two hundred foot tower.

"It is the most beautiful picnic park in all the Northwest. *It has unexcelled facilities to entertain Lodge, Club, Sunday School or Society picnics of any kind. Kitchens, toilet rooms, shelter houses, water supplies, all include the best and latest improvements for comfort and convenience,"* wrote A.W. Warnock, TCRT General Passenger Agent.

Passengers arriving on one of the huge ferryboats

The new tourists came, and they came by the thousands! They were encouraged by the Twin City Rapid Transit Company's new streetcar line from Minneapolis / St. Paul to Excelsior and Hill's new Great Northern train depot in Wayzata. *They had arrived in Excelsior by streetcar,* transferred to a 1000 passenger ferryboat, ridden the two miles to Big Island and now were standing on the dock deciding which way to go. Perhaps they had come with a group, maybe with a few friends, possibly this was a family or they might be a young couple on their first outing. In any event there was much to see and do. They moved quickly away, eager to explore and discover some of the Big Island wonders. Paths led them from the docks and towards the picnic and amusement areas.

(77)

A great place to picnic!

Big Island Park was developed as a recreational location for thousands of visitors from nearby Minneapolis and St. Paul. It was Twin City Lines intention to make the park strictly a family resort and a place to enjoy a summer day's picnic, whether for a few hours or an entire day. They built some unique architectural features throughout the island, and of these, probably the most novel was the *peristyle,* following the ridge of the island. It was built of concrete and outlined with electric lights. **Shown here on the left, the two hundred foot tower was also built of steel and concrete,** and was perhaps the most unusual structure on the island, in that it was a close copy of the famous tower of Seville, Spain. It contained the island's water supply, and at night was beautifully illuminated with hundreds of lights, and like a beacon, could be seen from all parts of the lake. The powerful beacon helped to guide the three huge passenger ferryboats to and from the park and to periodic weekend band concerts. **The postcard at the right shows the grassy mall between the landing and the tower.** The low building on the left contains the amusement arcade, and later, a large bird aviary. All of the buildings on the island are constructed in Spanish Mission architectural style and were exceedingly attractive. They included modern toilets and four picnic kitchens that groups could use for shelter and cooking. A number of amusement features were also built: a roller coaster, an old mill ride, a scenic ride through Yellowstone Park and in addition, there was a Pennyodeon, a Fun Factory and other activities.

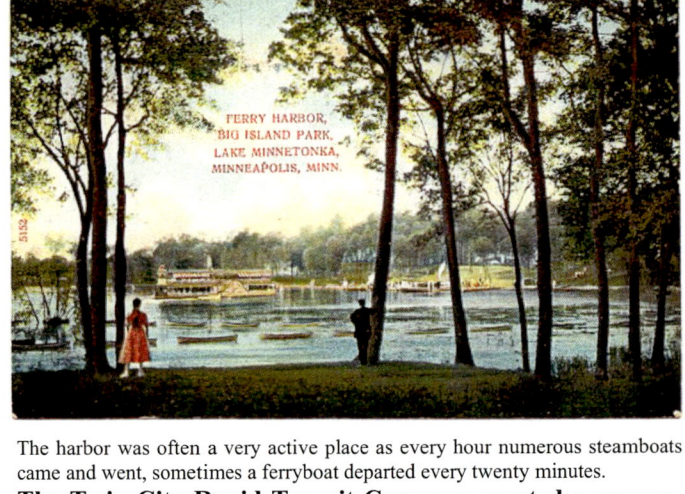

The harbor was often a very active place as every hour numerous steamboats came and went, sometimes a ferryboat departed every twenty minutes. **The Twin City Rapid Transit Company wanted a convenient, interesting attraction** for local and Twin City residents who were looking for an inexpensive outing. Near the electric tower were two modern picnic kitchen shelters both of Spanish Mission architecture. They were equipped with drinking water, stoves, ice, storage and picnic tables. Church, family or fraternal groups large or small could reserve these kitchens in advance. Ice and fuel was offered free of charge. There was a baseball diamond available for larger groups and swimming was also permitted in a designated area.

Left: This is the area in front of the tower that leads to the main dock and ferryboat landing. It was well lighted at night and was often a gathering place during the day.

There were at least two concerts everyday. A number of local bands were very popular. They included the Banda Rossa, the Navassar Ladies' Band and "Nelson and his Band" with Twin City vocalists. There were also periodic "lecturers" which added to the park's popularity. The park had an employee kitchen and men and women dormitories that housed a sizable staff.

Rowing with your best girlfriend on a sunny Sunday afternoon was fun and very popular. Sixty five hourly rental rowboats were available.

Rental rowboats

The grounds required a good deal of maintenance and provided jobs to a number of locals from Excelsior and around the lake.

Everyone wore their Sunday best

(78)

The Music Casino & John Phillip Sousa

Summer Band Concerts!....

The path through the Pergola to the Music Casino

The parks main attraction was the Music Casino with seating for over 1500 comfortably. It was a very uniquely shaped structure that cost over $50,000 to construct of steel, cement and glass. Often street-car boats would provide special runs for cottagers. They would pick them up and bring them to the island for the concert. Following the concert they would return them to their homes around the lake.

When the park opened in early 1906, many of the permanent features had not yet been completed. The park was open during August for picnics and gatherings and a temporary pavilion was erected on the island. The permanent Music Casino was constructed during the following winter.

The Music Casino was located on the highest point of the island. It was reached after a short pleasant walk on a pathway from the dock area (the path is still there). It wound through a grassy knoll shaded by huge elm and oak trees.

There were benches provided outside the Casino as well as inside seating. Many people preferred to sit on the grass and enjoy the cool breezes while listening to the wonderful concerts. **It was felt that music should be incidental, and that there should be no special charge for it, just part of a relaxing day or evening at the island.**

An occasional lecturer and a periodic high class vaudeville act added to the park's popularity. In 1908 improvements included the addition of wire screen and glass to the Casino. Seating was accomplished with wooden folding chairs.

Maestro Innes and his orchestra were brought in from New York to play during the month of August. The orchestra was comprised of 60 musicians and presented a variety of concerts. Their presentations included classical, grand opera and rag-time selections. They gave daily concerts through the end of the season, which occurred in September.

Many people preferred to sit on benches or the grass outside the casino

Walking to the main picnic area, notice the long dresses and straw hats

Company promotional literature stated that the park abounded in beautifully wooded heights, shady sylvan dales, rolling lawns, grand old trees, inviting nooks and ravines; all forming an ideal retreat for those who loved the pleasure of a good old fashioned family or party picnic with all the comforts one could ask for.

Pergola on the way to the Music Casino

The approach to the Music Casino passed beneath an arbor-like structure that was called a *"pergola"* It had huge concrete columns that supported a wooden trellis covered with beautiful vines.

The Music Casino, also of Spanish Mission architecture was an attractive structure constructed of concrete and red clay tile. It was large and well suited for concerts with its sloped seating arrangement.

John Phillip Sousa's Band was one to the most popular in the nation and during this period, 1906/1911, old timers tell of a special performance conducted at Big Island by John Phillip Sousa himself. Other notable bands played at the Casino as well, and concerts became an important part of summer entertainment.

The bands stayed at local hotels and boarding houses near the island during their engagements. Residents therefore became acquainted with individual band members and some even got musical instruction from them. It was a period of prosperity for all, as the townspeople benefited directly from the increased number of boarders and visitors to their communities.

Midway in the 1911 season, the Twin City Rapid Transit Company abruptly announced its plan to closes the Big Island Amusement Park at the end of the season. "It was the end of an exciting era."

MOST FAMOUS LAKE OF THE NORTHWEST
BEAUTIFUL
BIG ISLAND PARK
LAKE MINNETONKA
TWIN CITY LINES
COMO
COMO

The Minnehaha

Streetcars on the Lake

Lake Minnetonka

A HISTORICAL INSIGHT

Steamboat MINNEHAHA

© By Jim Ogland, author of
"Picturing Lake Minnetonka"

DNALGO Enterprises Box 935 Wayzata, Mn 55391

Streetcars... on the Lake!

In 1905 the Twin City Rapid Transit Company (TCRT) announced an exciting new development for Lake Minnetonka. They planned to extend their present streetcar line from Lake Harriet in Minneapolis to Excelsior, build an Amusement Park on Big Island and a fleet of excursion, express and ferry boats.

Transportation was changing, both public and private. People were moving to the cities, and they were moving to Lake Minnetonka. *They could work in the city and live at the lake.* They did however, need good reliable transportation. The Twin City Rapid Transit Company saw the need and began plans to not only bring streetcars to the lake, but to extend lake transportation by building a fleet of fast yellow Express Boats that could quickly and reliably transport residents to all points on the lake.

The boats operated from 6:30am to 7:30 pm May 15th through September 1906/1926

Six *"Streetcar"* boats were initially built, with a seventh added in 1915. The boats were built for speed. Their unique torpedo stern was designed to leave a small wake as the boats swept in close to shore or through narrow channels. They were designed locally by Royal Moore, owner of the Moore Boat Works located in Wayzata. The large oak frames (ribs) were sawn in Wayzata, then transported to the streetcar barns in Minneapolis for assembly in the company shops at 31st and Nicollet. All six boats were built during the winter of 1905-06. Loaded on flat cars, they were taken to Excelsior for launching. Two of the boats were launched on May 2, 1906, to assist with the early opening of the new Big Island Amusement Park. They were the *Minnehaha and Stillwater*. The remaining boats were launched on May 7, 1906. Rather than being numbered like regular streetcars, they were named after routes on the Minneapolis / St. Paul streetcar lines. They were: *White Bear, Como, Harriet, Stillwater, Minnehaha, Hopkins and Excelsior.* They were painted the same canary yellow as their streetcar cousins. Trim colors of olive green with oxide red were also the same. The interiors were almost identical. Cane-seats and benches,

Almost identical interiors as their streetcar cousins

with bronze hardware filled the cabin. Streetcar drop down windows and light fixtures were used throughout. The boats were 70 feet long and 14ft 10 inches wide. **They had a sleek appearance and very quickly became the darlings of the lake.** The upper deck had thirteen benches which accommodated about seventy passengers. Upper deck canopies were added five years later in 1911. This gave passengers additional protection from the sun and smokestack soot, also making them more of an all weather boat. The boats were fast and ran on a very tight schedule allowing them to complete their routes and return hourly to Excelsior. They had regular stops, but would stop at most any dock if signaled.

Big Island Amusement Park often had music concerts on summer nights. The streetcar boats would pick up cottagers and bring them to the concerts and at the end of the evening return them to their homes. The boats had a three man crew consisting of the Captain or Pilot who was an experienced seaman and knew his boat and the lake well. The Engineer took charge of the six ton steam engine and boiler and carried out bell signals from the Captain. A Purser collected tickets and handled lines when docking. In the winter, most crews worked on the Minneapolis / St. Paul streetcar lines.

Minnehaha steams on to its next stop somewhere in the Upper Lake. They could travel at 12 mph.

Passengers enjoyed the cabin's large open windows.

(84)

Six Fast *Express Boats*
White Bear Como Harriet Stillwater Minnehaha Hopkins

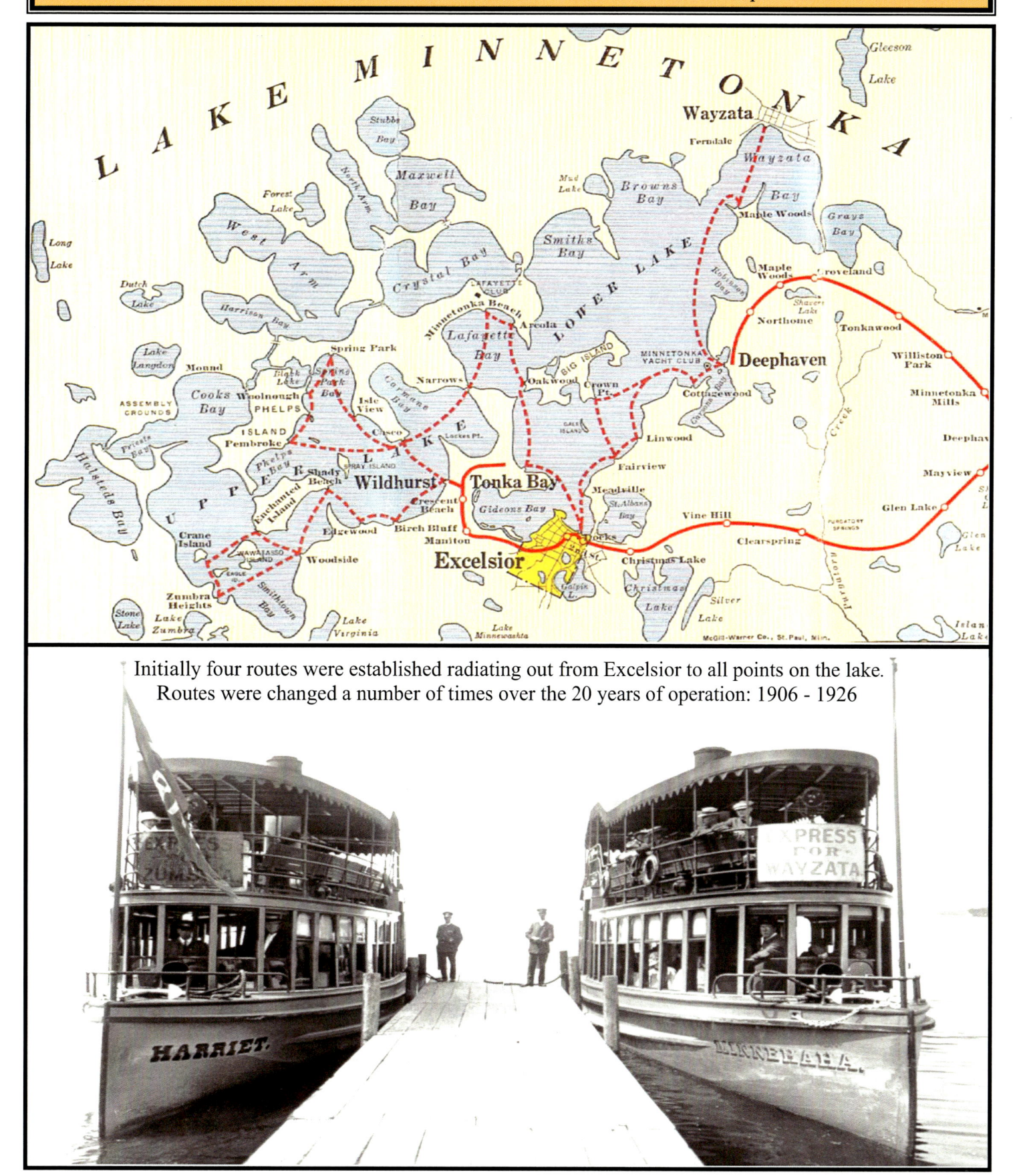

Initially four routes were established radiating out from Excelsior to all points on the lake. Routes were changed a number of times over the 20 years of operation: 1906 - 1926

Dismantled - *Sunk* - 1926

The exciting new boats were fun, they were unique, unusual and eye-catching with their torpedo sterns, bright yellow color, upper deck benches, cane seats, sharp bows and streetcar-like appearance. Residents and visitors alike loved the "yellow jackets" as they were often affectionately referred to. **The Minnehaha and her sisters quickly became the darlings of the lake.** Their reign was over all too quickly.

By the middle 1920's, Henry Ford's Model T and other automobiles had become the preferred mode of transportation. Ridership on the steamboats was at an all time low, resulting in frequent schedule changes, with only two routes remaining. In July 1926, after only two months of operation with two boats still operating, service was finally discontinued. Three boats: the *Como, White Bear* and the *Minnehaha* were dismantled. They were filled with red clay tile from the demolished Big Island Amusement Park, then towed to deep water between Big Island and Brackett"s Point, filled with water and unceremoniously sunk.

The *Stillwater* and *Harriet* were also dismantled the same year. The streetcar boat, *Excelsior*, was converted to a tug. In 1927, the *Hopkins* was sold to the Blue Line Café, painted white and renamed the *Minnetonka*. It was used as an excursion boat until 1949 when it was also scuttled and sunk in the same area. It has been video taped and appears to be in good condition.

Four Express Boats at their home dock in Excelsior

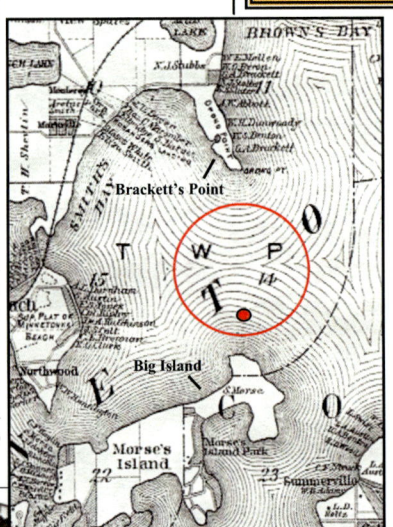

Waiting for the next boat, notice baby with camera.

Above: Approximate position of the sunken Minnehaha. Located about 900 yards off the northernmost tip of Big Island in 65ft of deep water. Photo on the left is the *Hopkins*, later re-named the *Minnetonka*. Notice the flamingo on the foredeck and awnings on the side. Its coal fired boiler and steam engine were converted to diesel.

Search and Discovery

In 1975, Jerry Provost, a local resident and professional underwater diver, became interested in searching for and possibly locating one of the sunken Minnetonka streetcar boats. They had been on the bottom for almost 50 years and Jerry thought it would be great to bring one up for the nation's 200th year Bicentennial Celebration in 1976.

Gathering information from various sources, he began to get a general idea of where the boats had been sunk. Everything indicated they were in deep water just north of Big Island on a line with Brackett's Point. He began some exploratory dives with little success. The search became an obsession, days turned into weeks and weeks into months. He found a lot of things on the bottom, but no boats. It became clear that they would not find a boat for the Bicentennial. Even with the addition of Lorance sonar equipment, acquired in 1977, nothing showed up. **A breakthrough came in the late fall of 1978.** While flying over the lake a pilot friend reported spotting a dark silhouette in the water north of Big Island. Jerry immediately, in his own airplane, flew over the area and confirmed the sighting. Unfortunately, within a few days winter set in and the lake froze over. A few dives through the ice brought no results. New deep water helmets had been purchased for a big underwater job in North Dakota. It was decided to check them out with an early spring dive in Lake Minnetonka. Returning to the spot of the silhouette, one of Jerry's friends suited up and descended to the bottom, landing right on the deck of a large wooden boat. It appeared to be about 70ft long and was almost completely buried in the mud. The bow flag mast was still there as was the boat's wooden steering wheel. This was unbelievable! **No name was visible on the exposed hull, but it definitely was a streetcar boat.** The long search was finally over. . . .

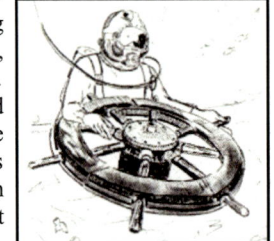

Diver with the steering wheel

(86)

Up from the *depths* . . .

Diving as much as possible continued throughout the fall of 1979. Collecting artifacts and surveying the soundness of the hull took much of the time. Despite being on the bottom for 54 years, the hull was in remarkable shape. Sinking so deep into the mud apparently had helped to preserve the cypress planking. Plans were beginning to shape up for possibly raising the boat the following summer of 1980. In the spring and early summer, after removing hundreds of pounds of debris from inside the hull, it was decided to make an attempt at raising the boat on Monday, August 25th. **Bill Niccum, owner of the Minnetonka Portable Dredging Company had offered his equipment to help in anyway that might be needed.** Niccum arranged for a large steel barge to be positioned over the hull and used as a dive/work platform. After removing more concrete, red tile and other debris from the hull, eight large airbags were to be attached with straps around the hull. To get the straps in position required a lot of dredging under the hull with high pressure hoses and pumps. This was dangerous work in 60ft of dark water and required seasoned professional divers to complete the job. The more experienced hardhat divers worked on the under-hull dredging, while the less experienced SCUBA divers continued to remove debris from inside the hull. Once the dredging was done and the bags in place, inflation could begin. Each bag was capable of lifting 2000lbs, a total of 16,000 pounds of lift. **The airbags were inflated, but the boat didn't move. Repositioning the bags didn't help. The deep mud was causing too much suction. On Wednesday, August 27th:** Niccum brought out a small barge-mounted crane to assist in freeing the boat from the mud in which it was deeply mired. This helped a little but it was still not breaking free. Tomorrow, Niccum, will bring out another barge and another crane. **Thursday August 28th:** With two cranes in place the bow finally broke free, but the stern dug in deeper and some of the straps slipped off. Divers worked all day dredging and repositioning airbags and straps. **On the 5th day, Friday August 29th:** Large spectator crowds gathered in their boats to watch the effort being made to raise a piece of history. **A 3rd barge and a 3rd huge crane were brought out and were now in place.** Late in the day everything was ready for a final try. All the cranes began lifting and pulling. Finally the boat broke free and was slowly coming to the surface. With increasing thunder and lightning and a fast approaching electrical storm, it was important to move the hull closer to Big Island and to more shallow water. As the tugs pushed the barges towards shore, the hull broke thru the surface and began to appear. The spectator crowd went crazy. Whistles, horns and sirens were blowing, people were screaming and yelling. **What a moment! What an effort!** Once the heavy debris was cleaned out, it floated on its own without the aid of the cranes or airbags. It looked much larger than anyone thought it would.

The boat was temporarily blocked up and stored in the dredging company yard until a decision could be made on how to proceed. As the planking began to dry out, a name gradually appeared on the bow of the boat. **It was the MINNEHAHA.** It attracted great public interest and literally hundreds of people filed by to look at it. About this time, the State of Minnesota laid claim to the boat stating that everything recovered from the bottom of the lake became state property. After four years, ownership was finally resolved, and the title was acquired by the "Inland Lake Interpretive Center," a non profit group formed to promote the boat restoration. Money was difficult to raise. Interest had waned and the unprotected boat, exposed to the elements and weather for ten years, was rapidly deteriorating. It could not take another year. In addition, space in the dredging yard was needed. Something would have to be done, and done soon!

A *Second* Chance

In the early spring of 1990, a local resident, Leo Meloche, recently retired from IBM, decided to do something about it. He gathered a few others together whom he thought would be interested in helping save the Minnehaha and to put an operating steamboat back on Lake Minnetonka. **The plan that this small group implemented would eventually take six years, hundreds of volunteer man hours and thousands of dollars to complete.** One of the first things needed was a building to house and protect the boat while providing space to begin a huge restoration. **A "second chance" was generously given by Jim and Jo Ann Jundt who paid for a building to be built at 140 George Street in Excelsior.** The site for the building was perfect. It was very close to the trail that led to the dredging yard where the boat was stored. The land for it was donated by the Hennepin County Regional Railroad Authority. Funding a project such as this would be especially important and much of it would come from tax deductible contributions. The Minnesota Transportation Museum agreed to form a new Lake Minnetonka Steamboat Division and give the project a tax deductible non-profit status. The community was excited and totally supportive of this effort.

This is the double bitt on the front deck that shows the years of weathering.

(87)

Restoration

Steamboats sometimes seem to have charmed lives. **The Minnehaha was getting a second chance!** Plans soon began to totally restore the seventy foot streetcar boat and return it to service on the lake. **The restoration immediately attracted great interest throughout the community and the entire state.** Donations began to pour in and volunteers of all skill levels began to assemble. **A special, fourteen wheel trailer was built to cradle and transport the 35 ton hull.** A large ninety by forty foot, two story Lester metal building, was designed and constructed to house and protect the boat. In late fall the *Minnehaha* was moved to her new home.

After a thorough clearing of all debris in the hull, came the replacement of many deteriorated oak frames (ribs). These in turn were replaced with new, carefully laminated, three inch thick, steam-bent oak frames. They were initially glued into place and eventually permanently bolted to the hull planks with stainless steel bolts. Steadily month by month, volunteers continued skillfully fitting and replacing many of the two inch thick cypress hull planks. Stem and stern timbers were rebuilt. Others began framing and enclosing the main cabin. A new keel and keelson was also installed.

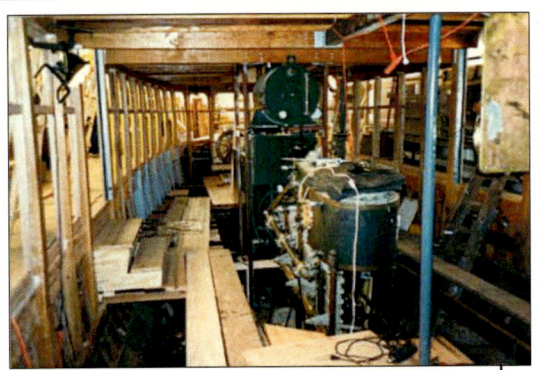

THE RESTORATION YEARS 1990 - 1996

- **1990** Title passes to the Minnesota Transportation Museum. A Steamboat Division is formed. A building is built in Excelsior to house the Minnehaha.
- **1991** Plans are developed, tools are acquired, schedules are established, volunteers begin work on the hull, replacing frames (ribs) and planking.
- **1992** Stem and stern timbers are rebuilt, a new keel and keelson are installed as are bilge stringers.
- **1993** Main cabin construction starts, steam engine and boiler are lifted into position.
- **1994** Cabin structure, windows, mechanical and electrical work, and painting continues.
- **1995** Cabin seats, canvas deck covering, upper deck benches, railing and lighting is installed. Brief in-the-water lake trials begin in mid summer.
- **1996 Maiden Voyage, May 25th** Minnehaha returns to passenger service on Lake Minnetonka after 70 years.

Donations began to find their way to the project. Not only needed operating cash, but pledges of support and original equipment came from all corners. A wooden spoke steering wheel from one of the original Express Boats was donated. Thirteen original upper deck benches were returned, as was an original 100 lb bow anchor. **A complete set of split cane interior cabin seats that had been stored in an Excelsior shopowner's basement were donated.** The original, brass bow search light came back, as did cleats, chocks, running lights and even a flag staff. 3M Corporation donated all of the paint, caulking, adhesives, brushes and sandpaper. Other generous mfgs. donated nuts, bolts, nails, glass, equipment and tools of all kinds.

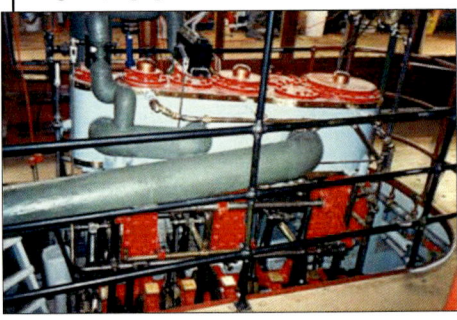

This 4 ton, triple expansion compounding steam engine (almost identical to the original) was acquired and installed during the restoration process. The steam engine, boiler and condensing unit alone weigh an estimated twelve tons. Precise location of this equipment along with the large fuel and water tanks and the installation of a heavy electrical motor generator was necessary for proper displacement and stability of the seventy foot, 35 ton Minnehaha.

In the days and weeks leading up to the Maiden Voyage, canvas banners such as the one on the right were hung on the light poles in the cities of Wayzata and Excelsior

"Steamboat a' Comin'"
1906 - 1996

Promotion and fund raising was very important during the restoration years and the response of the community was incredible. Several signed and numbered limited edition prints by artist Kurt Carlson were created and sold, as were a number of informative publications. Ten successful silent and live auction annual fund raising banquets were held at the Lafayette Club. **Since its return to service on the lake, over 13,000 passengers have ridden on the restored Minnehaha.**

Ready for Passengers

What started as an impossible dream was now a reality!
Literally from out of the depths has come one of the legendary streetcar boats of the "Roaring Twenties." It has captured the hearts and minds of all who have heard about her.

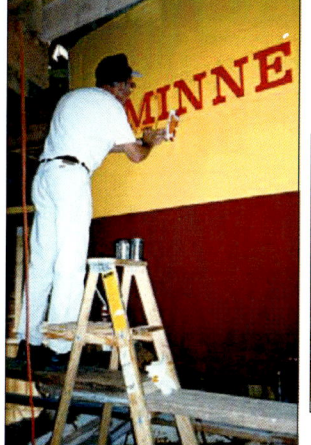

In the early fall of 1995, the *Minnehaha* was ready for sea trials. This would be the test of six years of restoration & countless man hours of crew training for engineers, pursers, pilots and captains. Electrical, mechanical and woodworking skills would be tested. **There were many questions, many unknowns. How would it handle? How fast would it be? How would it turn? How would it stop?**

Finishing touches!

Steamboat a'comin!
Returning from its successful first test run

Out of the barn 
With her newly caned wicker seats, glistening varnish on her interior trim, new recessed glass windows and polished brass, she was shipshape and had never looked better!

Forgotten and unremembered for over half a century, the now totally restored, bright yellow *Minnehaha* was decked out for this day—her day—her inaugural run from Excelsior to Wayzata. Vintage pennants were strung from the top of her stack to the bow and to the stern. With her whistles

Maiden Voyage 1996

Celebrating the Minnehaha's Maiden Voyage
It was an incredible event . . . After almost six years of restoration, anticipation and planning, the date was finally set! **May 25, 1996. Literally thousands of people turned out to watch as hundreds of boats with flags flying and horns blowing, escorted the *Minnehaha* across the lake from Excelsior to Wayzata.** . . . . The chance to celebrate the return of one of Minnetonka's legendary steamboats probably comes around only once in a lifetime. Those lucky enough to be on board for the Maiden Voyage, captured first-hand the thrill and the sound of the vintage steam whistle blowing long and loud as the *Minnehaha* backed smartly away from the Excelsior docks. Passengers in Turn-of-the-Century and Roaring Twenties period clothing re-lived for a moment the excitement and thrill of a day at the lake from so long ago.

Members of the crew. Ready to go and happy to be on board for this momentous occasion.

Promotional Button

Discover the Legend!

blowing and her new flags snapping sharply in the fresh morning breeze, all the thousands of painstaking restoration hours were focused on this moment. What a proud moment it was! Over 100 passengers had donated $1000 each to become Honorary Captains and to have a seat on the Maiden Voyage. After the formal champagne christening and remarks by local dignitaries, the "John Phillip Sousa Band" on board the "Lady of the Lake" excursion boat, struck up a lively march as the *Minnehaha* departed for Wayzata. Hundreds of spectators were gathered at the historic Wayzata Depot and for a later celebration at the Lafayette Country Club.

(89)

MINNEHAHA'S STEAM GAUGES

Postcards

The Golden Era of Postcards, 1907 - 1915

Lake Minnetonka

A HISTORICAL INSIGHT

LAKE MINNETONKA.

POSTCARDS

By Jim Ogland, author of
"Picturing Lake Minnetonka"

DNALGO Enterprises Box 935 Wayzata, Mn 55391

COLLECTING

A Brief History of Postcards

On May 13, 1873, United States government postcards first went on sale. They were purchased by businesses who had them imprinted with advertising messages and mailed to potential customers. *They became known as "advertising cards."* The first privately printed postcards in the United States were published in 1861, by H.L. Lipman of Philadelphia. *Picture postcards,* however, did not gain popularity until published at the **Chicago Worlds Columbian Exposition in 1893.** It was here that they became the earliest commercially produced picture postcards. Sold as "Souvenir Cards," they were an immediate success.

Government printed postcards could be mailed for one cent while privately printed cards required two cents.

By Act of Congress, May 19, 1898, privately printed postcards could now be mailed for the same postage as government cards. However, they had to conform to the same size and shape and *must bear the phrase,* **"Private Mailing Card."**

Finally, in 1901, Congress permitted "Post Card" to be printed on the backs of non-government cards, and in 1907, allowed the back to be divided with the address on one side and message on the other.

Collecting Postcards

Condition, rarity, view or subject, and to a lessor degree, age determines the value of any postcard.

It is helpful to be able to date a postcard even if it has not been used, though this does not necessarily mean an earlier card will be worth more than a newer card. For example, postcards published during the 1930's and 1940's are becoming more popular and valuable, as many middle aged people can identify with these images. This same gain in popularity can also be seen in postcards of the early Chrome Era (1945-1950's).

Postcards have been published in several eras from the mentioned 1860's until the present. Each publishing era has its own peculiarities which can help us to identify the age of a postcard. The following are the more prominent eras of early postcard publishing:

The Pioneer Card Era (1893-1898)

The Pioneer Era began when picture postcards were sold at the Columbian Exposition in Chicago in May of 1893. Their great success ensured that postcard collecting, then and now, would become a viable hobby. Pioneer cards are relatively scarce. They can be identified by distinctive features such as undivided backs, a Grant or Jefferson head stamp, and a postage of 2 cents. Other identifying characteristics include the fact that most are multiple view cards. The words *"Souvenir of" or "Greetings from"* appeared on many, and they are most commonly titled "Souvenir Card" or "Mail Card."

Private Mailing Card Era (1898-1901)

On December 24, 1901, Congress permitted "Post Card" to be printed on the backs of privately printed cards. However, these cards had undivided backs *and the user could write only the address on the back;* the message had to be written on the picture side of the card. For this reason, many of these cards have blank areas on the front for the writing.

The Divided Back Era (1907-1915)

On March 1, 1907, Congress followed the lead of several European nations and permitted postcards to be divided down the middle of the back, *making it possible for both the address and the message to be written there.* This prevented the face of the card from being marked, enhancing their collectibility. This *era saw an explosion of postcard publishing and is often referred to as the "GOLDEN AGE OF POST-CARDS."* Some printing techniques used in this era were expensive and high quality, but photography was still black and white. Better cameras and equipment, however, continued to improve the images that were being taken. Skilled artists hand colored postcards that were mostly printed in Europe, primarily Germany. With the advent of World War I, European postcard production came to an abrupt end.

(94)

POSTCARDS

By the turn of the century, the Glory Years at Lake Minnetonka had come to a close.

No longer would the lavish hotels and the magnificent steamboats of the 1880's dominate the lake. The wealthy tourist trade from the East and South had gone elsewhere.

The railroads were opening new frontiers. Automobiles were not here yet, but were just around the corner.

Soon there would be one of Henry Ford's Model T's in every garage.

Coincidentally it was the beginning of the *Golden Age of Postcards and the Golden Years at Lake Minnetonka.*

People were traveling, taking vacations, many for the first time. They were proud of where they were, and wanted to send something home. They wanted the people back home to know where they were and what fun they were having. *Postcards were perfect. Inexpensive, easy to use, people enjoyed them and the family back home loved receiving them.*

As the demand for postcards increased, publishers and promoters found a myriad of subjects to photograph. Lake Minnetonka was no exception. The hotel operators, large and small, each had their postcards. Photographers using large format view cameras (often 8x12 inch negatives or glass plates) frequently obtained exceptional black and white photos.

These photos of vacation areas, cities, towns, resorts and other scenic locations that people were visiting, soon became a pictorial record for the folks back home.

Color photography had not yet been developed. As a result, all colored postcards required hand coloring. This was accomplished by talented artists applying oil colors to the finished photos with cotton swabs or small, fine brushes.

In addition to local scenes, there were patriotic cards and holiday cards, such as the Fourth of July and New Years Day cards. Valentines' Day and hundreds of other romantic cards were extremely popular and were bought and mailed by the millions, to would be sweethearts every where.

Some local collections have in excess of over 500 known Lake Minnetonka postcards.

The back side or the written side of the card is often as interesting as the picture side. Proposals, wedding invitations, messages of all kinds are found on postcards. Cards were sometimes issued in sets with several different views of the same area or location. Many cards were purchased as simple souvenirs and often carried the phrase, "Souvenir of" or "Greetings from." Travelers often sent cards to themselves as a way of recording where they had been.

Some local studio photographers, recognizing the growing demand for views of popular resorts and scenic areas, soon began stockpiling images. One such firm was the Sweet Brothers, with studios located in Minneapolis. They produced hundreds of wonderful postcards of Lake Minnetonka.

Girls Wanted, Minneapolis,

One of the earliest hotels on the lake, the Chapman House, located on Cook's Bay in Mound, **opened with a bang on the Fourth of July, 1876.** It was a typical family summer resort with good food and great fishing. In 1906 a large pavilion was built which quickly became known as the Mound Casino and later as the popular **Surfside.**

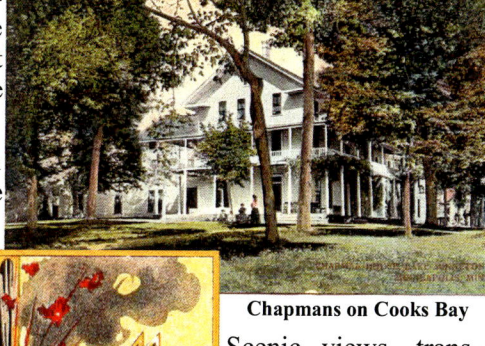

Chapmans on Cooks Bay

Scenic views, transportation, and hotels such as this Chapman card probably represent the majority of all the Lake Minnetonka cards.

Deltiology is the collecting of Postcards

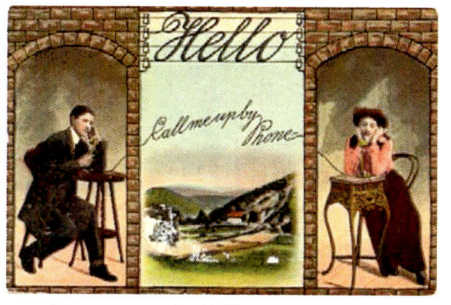

Romance cards of this type were very popular and thousands were produced.

Additional publishing eras

The White Border Era (1915-1930) Because of World War 1 and the end of European printing, the U.S. began printing postcards with white borders. Their poor quality resulted in an end to the postcard craze.

The Linen Era (1930-1945)

The Photochrome Era (1939-present)

The Real Photo Era (1901-Present)

STREETCARS IN THE CORNFIELDS

Minnetonka streetcars could hit speeds of sixty miles an hour. The distance to Excelsior from downtown Minneapolis was approximately 18 miles and could be covered in about 46 minutes.

It was an exhilarating ride to the lake. The fare was 25 cents, one way.

In the summer of 1906, streetcars began rolling westward from Minneapolis to Excelsior and Lake Minnetonka. With them came excited tourists and first time visitors to the lake looking for summer fun at the new amusement park. The route was often referred to as the "Great White Way" because of how brilliantly it was illuminated at night. It made night trips very unique and created a memory that lasted forever. At peak times on weekends and holidays there were often as many as sixty streetcars on the tracks going and coming at the same time.

This TCRT, (Twin City Rapid Transit) company brochure cover and the accompanying postcard were both published in 1907. The postcard, mailed on June 17, 1907, was a very popular one. After spending an entire day at the lake, people were often glad to be headed home.

The return trip was a chance to relax and enjoy the ride. As the streetcars picked up speed, they rhythmically swayed from side to side. Surprisingly the woven cane seats were quite comfortable. There were few stops and everyone was unusually quiet, even the children. **Streetcars also brought commuting residents to the city and early morning fishermen to the lake.** The first streetcar of the morning left downtown Minneapolis at 4:03 am. It was called the 'Early Bird Special" and was primarily for fishermen.

Residents of Excelsior awoke in the spring of 1905 to the pounding of spikes. Tracks were being laid on main street and soon to follow were bright yellow double-decker streetcars. **The Twin City Rapid Transit Company** played a major role during this exciting period. Thomas Lowry, the charismatic president of the sprawling streetcar company, recognized the need to develop destination points for people to visit, *and to give them some reason to ride his streetcars.* **That reason would be a new amusement park at Lake Minnetonka on Big Island.**

(96)

Lake Minnetonka VIEWS & SCENES

The Narrows Channel divides Lake Minnetonka into two distinct bodies-*the Upper Lake and the Lower Lake.* Each was formed by a different receding glacier thousands of years apart. Therefore each has many unique and different characteristics. Depths, shorelines, trees and aquatic life are very different in both. Vegetation and fish species are more abundant in one lake than the other. Lake Minnetonka is actually a combination of three of the four classifications of lakes in the world.

SPIRIT ISLAND, LAKE MINNETONKA, MINN.

Spirit Island in the distant upper left as viewed from the Ferndale area, was very important to the early American Indians. The entire Minnetonka area was significant to the spiritual life of the Dakota Indians. Ceremonies were held on Big Island as well as across the bay at Spirit Knob, on what later became known as Breezy Point. It was here that the Dakota came to hold their festivals and medicine rites.

ZUMBRO HEIGHTS, LAKE MINNETONKA.

Above: Zumbra Heights card is a good example of the 'White Border Era," cards, that were printed in the USA during World War I, (1915-1930.) It was said to be a way of saving on colored ink for the war effort.
The stop at Zumbra was the furthermost point on the Streetcar Boats regularly scheduled routes. Vacationers arrived on the Streetcar Boats to stay at the nearby **Palmer House.**

Hotel Edgewood was located on Birch Bluff in the Upper Lake and was a Streetcar Steamboat stop. Originally built by John Mann in the 1860's, it was a comfortable, small resort that catered to families and offered good home-cooked meals. There were plenty of fishing boats and guides if desired.

HOTEL EDGEWOOD, LAKE MINNETONKA, MINN.

Many sacred areas near the lake were also the sites of numerous burial grounds. Four hundred and ninety five burial mounds were identified around the lake. There were a number of large mounds, but most were small and dome shaped. The Dakota were able to keep the lake a secret from the White man for many years.

You can't see us for the dust at Crystal Bay, Minn.

Passing from Lower Lake into Crystal Bay, Lake Minnetonka.

These were more gentle and quieter times; no motor boats, no wakes, just ripples, with paddles or oars.

(97)

PLACES at Lake Minnetonka

BIG ISLAND AMUSEMENT PARK opened in the summer of 1906 with great fanfare and excitement. Weekends and holidays brought as many as 15,000 tourists a day to the park. The park was primarily designed as a picnic park catering to church groups and fraternal organizations. The Music Casino was a major attraction with numerous concerts at no cost. The first year big name bands, including John Phillip Sousa, were scheduled. The following years more local bands were employed. Among them was the Banda Rossa Orchestra.

One of the three huge 1000 passenger, 140 ft Ferryboats landing at the Big Island Amusement Park dock.

Casino and Walk Big Island Park, Lake Minnetonka, Minn.

WHEN WOMEN WORE WHITE DRESSES!
Renting a rowboat and rowing for a few hours with your favorite lady friend was very special and sometimes the bay was crowded with boats. Visitors dressed up in their Sunday best to come to the Island. Women wore white dresses and men wore suits and ties. Everyone had a hat. Ladies hats were large with floral pieces, ribbons and bows. Most of the men wore straw hats, called "boaters."

THE NEW NARROWS
The new Narrows is a channel that connects the Lower and the Upper Lakes. Previously, there was an earlier channel a few blocks to the south. It was long, weedy and shallow and didn't allow larger boats to pass thru it. A cable-drawn ferry was in use to cross the channel from 1857 to 1911, when a steel bridge was built.

The Narrows

Postcards are wonderful records of our historical and often colorful past. Although they may not have been intended as such, they often provide the only record of an event, an object or a location. The postcards themselves are treasures, but stamped, dated, and written-on postcards, add a second dimension to the photo on the other side.

Following the disastrous fire that destroyed James J. Hill's huge Hotel Lafayette in 1897, a nine hole golf course and a new smaller clubhouse (pictured on the right) was built in 1899 on the same property. Over the years, it was enlarged several times to eventually include a large dining room and a ballroom. It became the social center of Minnetonka Beach and the lake area. The new clubhouse was built to overlook Crystal Bay rather than Lafayette Bay, as the former one had. This card was mailed in 1922, the same year that this clubhouse also burned to the ground.

4325. Lafayette Club House, Minneapolis, Minn.

Lafayette Golf Club
1899-1922

(98)

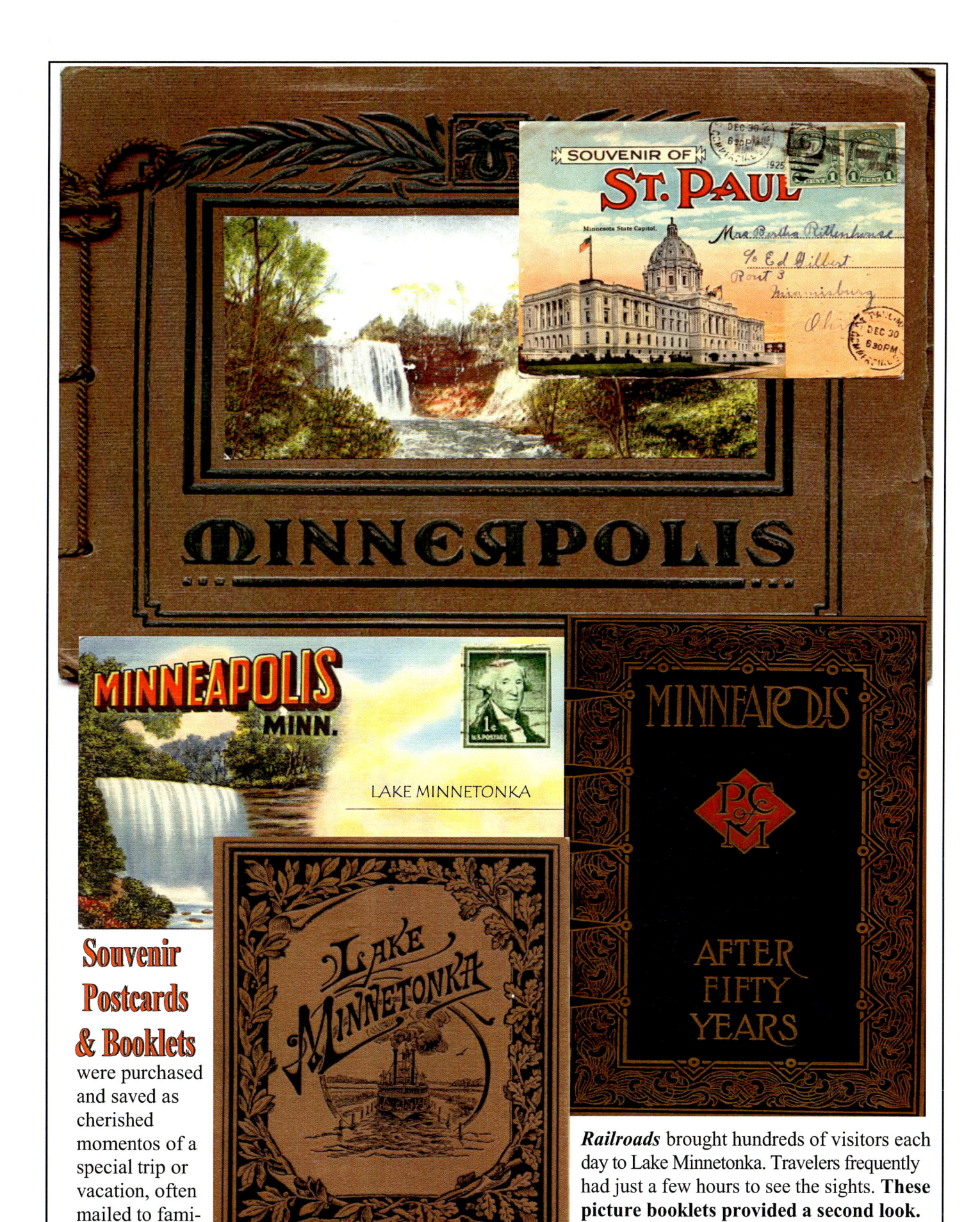

Souvenir Postcards & Booklets were purchased and saved as cherished momentos of a special trip or vacation, often mailed to families back home.

Railroads brought hundreds of visitors each day to Lake Minnetonka. Travelers frequently had just a few hours to see the sights. **These picture booklets provided a second look.**

(99)

LAKE MINNETONKA
Vintage Postcards

BIG ISLAND PARK, WHARVES, FERRY LANDING, LAKE MINNETONKA, MINN.

From the Turn of the Century

PAGE INDEX

Title Page

I Contents
II Introduction
III Preface
IV Early History
V Copyright Page

1 Historical Insights Collection
2 Blank
3 Historical Timeline Cover
4 Lake Minnetonka time line
5 Early history
6 Incredible Hotels
7 Big Island, Yacht Club
8 Glossary
9 Map, Lake Minnetonka
10 Timeline rear cover,
11 Divider Huge Hotels
12 Blank
13 Grand Hotels Cover
14 Hotels –Historic Insight
15 Lake Park Hotel
16 Lafayette Hotel
17 Hotel Del Otero
18 First of Grand Hotels, St. Louis
19 Over 60 Hotels
20 Lower Lake, Upper Lake
21 Divider Steamboatin'
22 Blank
23 Steamboats Cover
24 Steamboatin'
25 City of St. Louis
26 Minnetonka Steamers
27 Glory years, 1880's, 1890's
28 Tickets, Steamboats
29 Minnetonka Steamboats, list of
30 Big Island Ferrys
31 Divider Excelsior
32 Blank
33 Excelsior Cover
34 Historic Excelsior
35 Pioneers
36 Tourism
37 Excelsior Home Port

38 Golden Years, 1900 - 1930
39 Roaring Twenties
40 Apples, Rear Cover Excels
41 Wayzata Divider
42 Blank
43 Cover Ladies Wayzata
44 Wayzata
45 Pioneers / Settlers
46 Wayzata Theatre, train
47 Railroads, Boats
48 The Gilded Age
49 Turn of the Century
50 By the Waters, Sheet Music
51 Divider, Yachting
52 Blank
53 Yachting Cover
54 Yachting Timeline
55 Yachting was important
56 Yacht Club
57 Course Map
58 Ice boating
59 1920's 30's 40's
60 Yachting, Sailing Close
61 Divider, Mound
62 Blank
63 Mound Insight Cover
64 Mound Timeline
65 Early Settlement
66 Lodging Tourists
67 Steamers, Tours, Islands
68 Upper Lake
69 Roaring Twenties
70 Hiawatha
71 Divider, New Tourist
72 Blank
73 Big Island Cover
74 Historic Insights, Big Island
75 New Tourists
76 Park opens
77 By Streetcar, Train, by Boat
78 Great Place
79 Music Casino
80 Big Island Rear Cover
81 Divider Minnehaha
82 Blank

83 Minnehaha Cover
84 Streetcars
85 Fast Express Boats
86 Dismantled and sunk
87 Up from Depths
88 Restoration
89 Ready for passengers
90 Gauges
91 Divider Postcards
92 Blank
93 Postcards Cover
94 Collecting
95 Postcards
96 Streetcars in the Corn
97 Views & scenes
98 Places, Minnetonka
99 Booklets
100 Postcards Rear Cover
101 Index to Pages
102 Blank